Rudyard Kipling was born in Bom remained for the first five years o experiences, and his subsequent unhapp... England, inform much of his writing and his love of India can be seen throughout his work. In 1882 he returned to India where he worked as a journalist whilst also penning numerous short stories and poems, and it was not long before he found favour with the critics of the day. Hailed as a successor to Dickens, he went on to write some of his most famous novels, notably *The Jungle Book* and *Captains Courageous*. When tragedy struck his family with the death of his wife in 1899 followed by the death of his only son in 1915, his work inevitably took on a darker, more sombre tone and he remained preoccupied with the themes of psychological strain and breakdown until his death in 1936.

Kipling's reputation varied enormously both within his lifetime and in subsequent years. At one time hailed a genius – indeed Henry James called him 'the most amazing man of genius I have ever known' – and awarded the Nobel Prize for Literature, he later became increasingly unpopular with his paternalistic and colonial views being seen as unfashionable in the extreme. However, the enduring appeal of works such as *Kim*, *The Just So Stories*, and *The Jungle Books* has done much to redress the balance in recent years and he is once again regarded as the outstanding author that he is.

COLLECTED DOG STORIES

BY RUDYARD KIPLING

HOUSE OF
STRATUS

This edition published in 2001 by House of Stratus, an imprint of
Stratus Holdings plc, 24c Old Burlington Street, London, W1X 1RL, UK.

www.houseofstratus.com

Typeset, printed and bound by House of Stratus.

A catalogue record for this book is available from the British Library.

ISBN 1-84232-940-5

CONTENTS

PRIVATE LEAROYD'S STORY
And he told a tale – *Chronicles of Gautama Buddha.*

Far from the haunts of Company Officers who insist upon kit inspections, far from keen-nosed Sergeants who sniff the pipe stuffed into the bedding roll, two miles from the tumult of the barracks, lies the Trap. It is an old dry well, shadowed by a twisted *pipal* tree and fenced with high grass. Here, in the years gone by, did Private Ortheris establish his depot and menagerie for such possessions, dead and living, as could not safely be introduced to the barrack room. Here were gathered Houdin pullets, and fox terriers of undoubted pedigree and more than doubtful ownership, for Ortheris was an inveterate poacher and pre-eminent among a regiment of neat-handed dog stealers.

Never again will the long lazy evenings return wherein Ortheris, whistling softly, moved surgeon-wise among the captives of his craft at the bottom of the well; when Learoyd sat in the niche, giving sage counsel on the management of 'tykes', and Mulvaney, from the crook of the overhanging *pipal,* waved his enormous boots in benediction above our heads, delighting us with tales of Love and War, and strange experiences of cities and men.

Ortheris – landed at last in the 'little stuff' bird-shop' for which your soul longed; Learoyd – back again in the smoky, stone-ribbed North, amid the clang of the Bradford looms; Mulvaney – grizzled, tender, and very wise Ulysses, sweltering

1

on the earthwork of a Central India line—judge if I have forgotten old days in the Trap!

Orth'ris, as allus thinks he knaws more than other foaks, said she wasn't a real laady, but nobbut a Hewrasian. I don't gainsay as her culler was a bit doosky like. But she *was* a laady. Why, she rode iv a carriage, an' good 'osses, too, an' her 'air was that oiled as you could see your faice in it, an' she wore di'mond rings an' a goold chain, an' silk an' satin dresses as mun 'a' cost a deal, for it isn't a cheap shop as keeps enough o' one pattern to fit a figure like hers. Her naame was Mrs DeSussa, an' t' waay I coom to be acquainted wi' her was along of our Colonel's Laady's dog Rip.

I've seen a vast o' dogs, but Rip was t' prettiest picter of a cliver fox tarrier 'at iver I set eyes on. He could do owt yo' like but speeak, an' t' Colonel's Laady set more store by him than if he hed been a Christian. She hed bairns iv her awn, but they was i' England, and Rip seemed to get all t' coodlin' and pettin' as belonged to a bairn by good right.

But Rip wor a bit on a rover, an' hed a habit o' breakin' out o' barricks like, and trottin' round t' plaice as if he were t' Cantonment Magistrate coom round inspectin'. The Colonel leathers him once or twice, but Rip didn't care an' kept on gooin' his rounds, wi' his taail a-waggin' as if he were flag-signallin' to t' world at large 'at he was 'gettin' on nicely, thank yo', and how's yo'sen? An' then t' Colonel, as was noa sort of a hand wi' a dog, tees him oop. A real clipper iv a dog, an it's noa wonder yon laady, Mrs DeSussa, should tek a fancy tiv him. Theer's one o' t' Ten Commandments says yo' maun't cuvvet your neebor's ox nor his jackass, but it doesn't say nowt about his tarrier dogs, an' happen thot's t' reason why Mrs DeSussa cuvveted Rip, tho' she went to church reg'lar along wi' her husband who was so mich darker 'at if he hedn't such a good coaat tiv his back yo' might ha' called him a black man and nut tell a lee nawther. They said he addled his brass i' jute, an' he'd a rare lot on it.

2

Well, yo' see, when they teed Rip oop, t' poor awd lad didn't enjoy very good 'ealth. So t' Colonel's Laady sends for me as 'ad a naame for bein' knowledgeable about a dog, an' axes what's ailin' wi' him.

'Why,' says I, 'he's getten t' mopes, an' what he wants is his libbaty an' coompany like t' rest on us; wal happen a rat or two 'ud liven him oop. It's low, mum,' says I, 'is rats, but it's t' nature iv a dog; an' soa's cootin' round an' meetin' another dog or two an' passin' t' time o' day, an' hevvin' a bit on a turn-up wi' him like a Christian.'

So she says *her* dog maun't niver fight an' noa Christians iver fought.

'Then what's a soldier for?' says I; an' I explains to her t' contrairy qualities of a dog, 'at, when yo' coom to think on't, is one o' t' curusest things as is. For they larn to behave their-sens like gentlemen born, fit for t' fost o' coompany – they tell me t' Widdy herself is fond of a good dog and knaws one when she sees it as well as onny body: then on t' other hand a-tewin' round after cats an' gettin' mixed oop i' all manners o' blackguardly street rows, an' killin' rats, an' fightin' like divils.

T' Colonel's Laady says: – 'Well, Learoyd, I doan't agree wi' yo', but yo're right in a way o' speeakin', an' I should like yo' to tek Rip out a-walkin' wi' you sometimes; but yo' maun't let him fight, nor chaase cats, nor do nowt 'orrid': an' them was her very wods.

Soa Rip an' me gooes out a-walkin' o' evenin's, he bein' a dog as did credit tiv a man, an' I catches a lot o' rats an' we hed a bit of a match on in an awd dry swimmin'-bath at back o' t' cantonments, an' it was none so long afore he was as bright as a button again. He hed a way o' flyin' at them big yaller pariah dogs as if he was a harrow offan a bow, an' though his weight were nowt, he tuk 'em so suddint-like they rolled over like skittles in a halley, an' when they coot he stretched after 'em as if he were rabbit-runnin'. Saame wi' cats when he cud get t' cat agaate o' runnin'.

3

One evenin', him an' me was trespassin' ovver a compound wall after one of them mongooses 'at he'd started, an' we was busy grubbin' round a prickle-bush, an' when we looks oop there was Mrs DeSussa wi' a parasel ovver her shoulder a-watchin' us. 'Oh my!' she sings out; 'There's that lovelee dog! Would he let me stroke him, Mister Soldier?'

'Ay, he would, mum,' says I, 'for he's fond o' laadies' coompany. Coom here, Rip, an' speeak to this kind laady.' An' Rip, seein' 'at t' mongoose hed getten clean awaay, cooms oop like t' gentleman he was, niver a hauporth shy nor okkord.

'Oh, you beautiful – you prettee dog!' she says, clippin' an chantin' her speech in a waay them sooart has o' their awn; 'I would like a dog like you. You are so verree lovelee – so awfullee prettee,' an' all thot sort o' talk, 'at a dog o' sense mebbe thinks nowt on, tho' he bides it by reason o' his breedin'.

An' then I meks him joomp ovver my swagger-cane, an' shek hands, an' beg, an' lie dead, an' a lot o' them tricks as laadies teeaches dogs, though I doan't haud wi' it mysen; for it's makin' a fool o' a good dog to do suchlike.

An' at lung length it cooms out 'at she'd been thrawin' sheep's eyes, as t' sayin' is, at Rip for many a day. Yo' see, her childer was grown up, an' she'd nowt mich to do, an' were allus fond of a dog. Soa she axes me if I'd tek somethin' to drink. An' we gooes into t' drawn room wheer her 'usband was a-settin'. They meks a gurt fuss ovver t' dog an' I has a bottle o' aale an' he gev me a handful o' cigars.

Soa I coomed awaay, but t' awd lass sings out – 'Oh, Mister Soldier, please coom again and bring that prettee dog.'

I didn't let on to t' Colonel's Laady about Mrs DeSussa, an' Rip, he says nowt nawther; an' I gooes again, an' ivry time there was a good dhrink an' a handful o' good smoaks. An' I telled t' awd lass a heeap more about Rip than I'd ever heeard; how he tuk t' fost prize at Lunnon dog show an' cost thotty-three pounds fower shillin' from t' man as bred him; 'at his own brother was t' propputty o' t' Prince o' Wailes, an' 'at he had a pedigree as long as a Dook's. An' she lapped it all oop an' wor niver tired o' admirin' him. But when t' awd lass took to givin' me money an' I seed 'at she wor gettin' fair fond about t' dog, I began to suspicion summat. Onny body may give a soldier t' price of a pint in a friendly waay an' theer's no 'arm done, but when it cooms to five rupees slipt into your hand, sly like, why, it's what t' 'lectioneerin' fellows calls bribery an' corruption. Specially when Mrs DeSussa threwed hints how t' cold weather would soon be ovver, an' she was gooin' to Munsooree Pahar an' we was gooin' to Rawalpindi, an' she would niver see Rip onny more onless somebody she knawed on would be kind tiv her.

Soa I tells Mulvaney an' Orth'ris all t' taale thro', beginnin' to end.

''Tis larceny that wicked ould laady manes,' says t' Irishman, ''tis felony she is sejucin' ye into, my frind Learoyd, but I'll purtect your innocince. I'll save ye from the wicked wiles av that wealthy ould woman, an' I'll go wid ye this evenin' an' spake to her the wurrds av truth an' honesty. But, Jock,' says he, waggin' his heead, ''twas not like ye to kape all that good dhrink an' thim fine cigars to yerself, while Orth'ris here an' me have been prowlin' round wid throats as dry as limekilns, and nothin' to smoke but Canteen plug. 'Twas a dhirty thrick to play on a comrade, for why should you, Learoyd, be balancin' yerself on the butt av a satin chair, as if Terence Mulvaney was not the aquil av anybody who thrades in jute!'

'Let alone me,' sticks in Orth'ris, 'but that's like life. Them wot's really fitted to decorate society get no show, while a blunderin' Yorkshireman like you –'

'Nay,' says I, 'it's none o' t' blunderin' Yorkshireman she wants. It's Rip. He's t' gentleman this journey.'

Soa t' next day, Mulvaney an' Rip an' me gooes to Mrs DeSussa's, an' t' Irishman bein' a strainger she wor a bit shy at fost. But yo've heeard Mulvaney talk, an' yo' may believe as he fairly bewitched t' awd lass wal she let out 'at she wanted to tek

5

Rip awaay wi' her to Munsooree Pahar. Then Mulvaney changes his tune an' axes her solemn-like if she'd thowt o' t' consequences o' gettin' two poor but honest soldiers sent t' Andamning Islands. Mrs DeSussa began to cry, so Mulvaney turns round oppen t' other tack and smooths her down, allowin' 'at Rip ud be a vast better off in t' Hills than down i' Bengal, an' 'twor a pity he shouldn't go wheer he was so well beliked. And soa he went on, backin' an' fillin' an' workin' up t' awd lass wal she felt as if her life warn't worth nowt if she didn't hev t' dog.

Then all of a suddint he says: – 'But ye *shall* have him, marm, for I've a feelin' heart, not like this cowld-blooded Yorkshireman; but 'twill cost ye not a penny less than three hundher rupees.'

'Don't yo' believe him, mum,' says I; 't' Colonel's Laady wouldn't tek five hundred for him.'

'Who said she would?' says Mulvaney; 'it's not buyin' him I mane, but for the sake o' this kind, good laady, I'll do what I never dreamt to do in my life. I'll stale him!'

'Don't say steal,' says Mrs DeSussa; 'he shall have the happiest home. Dogs often get lost, you know, and then they stray, an' he likes me an' I like him as I niver liked a dog yet, an' I *must* hev him. If I got him at t' last minute I could carry him off to Munsooree Pahar and nobody would niver knaw.'

Now an' again Mulvaney looked acrost at me, an' though I could mek nowt o' what he was after, I concluded to tek his leead.

'Well, mum,' I says, 'I never thowt to coom down to dog-steealin', but if my comraade sees how it could be done to oblige a laady like yo'sen, I'm nut t' man to hod back, tho' it's a bad business I'm thinkin', an' three hundred rupees is a poor set-off again t' chance of them Damning Islands as Mulvaney talks on.'

'I'll mek it three-fifty,' says Mrs DeSussa. 'Onlee let me hev t' dog!'

So we let her persuade us, an' she teks Rip's measure theer an' then, an' sent to Hamilton's to order a silver collar again t' time when he was to be her awn, which was to be t' day she set off for Munsooree Pahar.

'Sitha, Mulvaney,' says I, when we was outside, 'yo're niver goin' to let her hev Rip!'

'An' wud ye disappoint a poor old woman?' says he. 'She shall have *a* Rip.'

'An' wheer's he to come through?' says I.

'Learoyd, my man,' he sings out, 'you're a pretty man av your inches an' a good comrade, but your head is made av duff. Isn't our frind Orth'ris a Taxidermist, an' a rale artist wid his nimble white fingers? An' fwhat's a Taxidermist but a man who can thrate shkins? Do ye mind the white dog that belongs to the Canteen Sargint, bad cess to him – he that's lost half his time an' snarlin' the rest? He shall be lost for *good* now; an' do ye mind that he's the very spit in shape an' size av the Colonel's, barrin' that his tail is an inch too long, an' he has none av the colour that divarsifies the rale Rip, an' his timper is that av his masther an' worse. But fwhat is an inch on a dog's tail? An' fwhat to a professional like Orth'ris is a few ringstraked shpots av black, brown, an' white? Nothin' at all, at all.'

Then we meets Orth'ris, an' that little man, bein' sharp as a needle, seed his way through t' business in a minute. An' he went to work a-practisin' 'air-dyes the very next day, beginnin' on some white rabbits he hed, an' then he drored all Rip's markin's on t' back of a white Commissariat bullock, so as to get his 'and in an' be sure of his cullers; shadin' off brown into black as nateral as life. If Rip *hed* a fault it was too mich markin', but it was straingely reg'lar, an' Orth'ris settled himself to make a fost-rate job on it when he got hand o' t' Canteen Sargint's dog. Theer niver was sich a dog as thot for bad temper, an' it did nut get no better when his tail hed to be fettled an inch an' a half shorter. But they may talk o' theer Royal Academies as they like. *I* niver seed a bit o' animal paintin' to beat t' copy as Orth'ris made of Rip's marks, wal t' picter itself was snarlin' all t' time an' tryin' to get at Rip standin' theer to be copied as good as goold.

Orth'ris allus hed as mich conceit on himsen as would lift a balloon, an' he wor so pleeased wi' his sham Rip he wor for tekkin' him to Mrs DeSussa before she went awaay. But Mulvaney an' me stopped thot, knowin' Orth'ris's work, though niver so cliver, was nobbut skin-deep.

An' at last Mrs DeSussa fixed t' day for startin' to Munsooree Pahar. We was to tek Rip to t' staashun i' a basket an' hand him ovver just when they was ready to start, an' then she'd give us t' brass – as was agreed upon.

An' my wod! It wor high time she wor off, for them 'air-dyes upon t' cur's back took a vast of paintin' to keep t' reet culler, tho' Orth'ris spent a matter o' seven rupees six annas i' t' best drooggist shops i' Calcutta.

An' t' Canteen Sargint was lookin' for 'is dog everywheer; an', wi' bein' teed oop, t' beast's timper got waur nor iver.

It wor i' t' evenin' when t' train started thro' Howrah, an' we 'elped Mrs DeSussa wi' about sixty boxes, an' then we gave her t' basket. Orth'ris, for pride iv his work, axed us to let him coom along wi' us, an' he couldn't help liftin' t' lid an' showin' t'cur as he lay coiled oop.

'Oh!' says t' awd lass; 'the beautee! How sweet he looks!' An' just then t' beauty snarled an' showed his teeth, so Mulvaney shuts down t' lid an' says: 'Ye'll be careful, marm, whin ye tek him out. He's disaccustomed to travellin' by t' railway, an' he'll be sure to want his rale mistress an' his frind Learoyd, so ye'll make allowance for his feelin's at fost.'

She would do all thot an' more for the dear, good Rip, an' she would nut oppen t' basket till they were miles away, for fear onny body should recognise him, an' we wor real good an' kind soldier-men, we wor, an' she honds me a bundle o' notes, an' then cooms oop a few of her relations an' friends to say goodbye – not more than seventy-five there wasn't – an' we coots awaay.

8

What coom to t' three hundred an' fifty rupees? Thot's what I can scarcelins tell yo', but we melted it – we melted it. It was share an' share alike, for Mulvaney said: 'If Learoyd got hoult av Mrs DeSussa first, sure 'twas me that remimbered the Sargint's dog just in the nick av time, an' Orth'ris was the artist av janius that made a work av art out av that ugly piece av ill natur'. Yet, by way av a thank-offerin' that I was not led into felony by that wicked ould woman, I'll send a thrifle to Father Victor for the poor people he's always beggin' for.'

But me an' Orth'ris, he bein' Cockney an' I bein' pretty far north, did nut see it i' t' saame waay. We'd getten t' brass, an' we meaned to keep it. An' soa we did – for a short time.

Noa, noa, we niver heeard a wod more o' t' awd lass. Our Rig'mint went to Pindi, an' t' Canteen Sargint he got himself another tyke insteead o' t' one 'at got lost so reg'lar, an' was lost for good at last.

GARM – A HOSTAGE

One night, a very long time ago, I drove to an Indian military cantonment called Mian Mir to see amateur theatricals. At the back of the Infantry barracks a soldier, his cap over one eye, rushed in front of the horses and shouted that he was a dangerous highway robber. As a matter of fact he was a friend of mine, so I told him to go home before anyone caught him; but he fell under the pole, and I heard voices of a military guard in search of someone.

The driver and I coaxed him into the carriage, drove home swiftly, undressed him and put him to bed, where he waked next morning with a sore headache, very much ashamed. When his uniform was cleaned and dried, and he had been shaved and washed and made neat, I drove him back to barracks with his arm in a fine white sling, and reported that I had accidentally run over him. I did not tell this story to my friend's sergeant, who was a hostile and unbelieving person, but to his lieutenant, who did not know us quite so well.

Three days later my friend came to call, and at his heels slobbered and fawned one of the finest bull terriers – of the old-fashioned breed, two parts bull and one terrier – that I had ever set eyes on. He was pure white, with a fawn-coloured saddle just behind his neck, and a fawn diamond at the root of his thin whippy tail. I had admired him distantly for more than a year; and Vixen, my own fox terrier, knew him too, but did not approve.

''E's for you,' said my friend but he did not look as though he liked parting with him.

10

'Nonsense! That dog's worth more than most men, Stanley,' I said.

'' E's that an' more. 'Tention!'

The dog rose on his hind legs, and stood upright for a full minute.

'Eyes right!'

He sat on his haunches and turned his head sharp to the right. At a sign he rose and barked thrice. Then he shook hands with his right paw and bounded lightly to my shoulder. Here he made himself into a necktie, limp and lifeless, hanging down on either side of my neck. I was told to pick him up and throw him in the air. He fell with a howl, and held up one leg.

'Part o' the trick,' said his owner. 'You're goin' to die now. Dig yourself your little grave an' shut your little eye.'

Still limping, the dog hobbled to the garden edge, dug a hole and lay down in it. When told that he was cured he jumped out, wagging his tail, and whining for applause. He was put through half a dozen other tricks, such as showing how he would hold a man safe (I was that man, and he sat down before me, his teeth bared, ready to spring), and how he would stop eating at the word of command. I had no more than finished praising him when my friend made a gesture that stopped the dog as though he had been shot, took a piece of blue-ruled canteen-paper from his helmet, handed it to me and ran away, while the dog looked after him and howled. I read

Sir – I give you the dog because of what you got me out of. He is the best I know, for I made him myself, and he is as good as a man. Please do not give him too much to eat, and please do not give him back to me, for I'm not going to take him, if you will keep him. So please do not try to give him back any more. I have kept his name back, so you can call him anything and he will answer, but please do not give him back. He can kill a man as easy as anything, but please do not give him too much meat. He knows more than a man.

Vixen sympathetically joined her shrill little yap to the bull terrier's despairing cry, and I was annoyed, for I knew that a man who cares for dogs is one thing, but a man who loves one dog is quite another. Dogs are at the best no more than verminous vagrants, self-scratchers, foul feeders, and unclean by the law of Moses and Mohammed; but a dog with whom one lives alone for at least six months in the year; a free thing, tied to you so strictly by love that without you he will not stir or exercise; a patient, temperate, humorous, wise soul, who knows your moods before you know them yourself, is not a dog under any ruling.

I had Vixen, who was all my dog to me; and I felt what my friend must have felt, at tearing out his heart in this style and leaving it in my garden. However, the dog understood clearly enough that I was his master, and did not follow the soldier. As soon as he drew breath I made much of him, and Vixen, yelling with jealousy, flew at him. Had she been of his own sex, he might have cheered himself with a fight, but he only looked worriedly when she nipped his deep iron sides, laid his heavy head on my knee, and howled anew. I meant to dine at the Club that night, but as darkness drew in, and the dog snuffed through the empty house like a child trying to recover from a fit of sobbing, I felt that I could not leave him to suffer his first evening alone. So we fed at home, Vixen on one side and the stranger-dog on the other; she watching his every mouthful, and saying explicitly what she thought of his table manners, which were much better than hers.

It was Vixen's custom, till the weather grew hot, to sleep in my bed, her head on the pillow like a Christian; and when morning came I would always find that the little thing had braced her feet against the wall and pushed me to the very edge of the cot. This night she hurried to bed purposefully, every hair up, one eye on the stranger, who had dropped on a mat in a helpless, hopeless sort of way, all four feet spread out, sighing heavily. She settled her head on the pillow several times, to show her little airs and graces, and struck up her usual whiney sing-song before slumber. The stranger-dog softly edged towards me. I put out my hand and he licked it. Instantly my wrist was between Vixen's teeth, and her warning *aaarh!* said as plainly as speech that if I took any further notice of the stranger she would bite.

I caught her behind her fat neck with my left hand, shook her severely, and said:

'Vixen, if you do that again you'll be put into the veranda. Now, remember!'

She understood perfectly, but the minute I released her she mouthed my right wrist once more, and waited with her ears back and all her body flattened, ready to bite. The big dog's tail thumped the floor in a humble and peace-making way.

I grabbed Vixen a second time, lifted her out of bed like a rabbit (she hated that and yelled), and, as I had promised, set her out in the veranda with the bats and the moonlight. At this she howled. Then she used coarse language – not to me, but to the bull terrier – till she coughed with exhaustion. Then she ran round the house trying every door. Then she went off to the stables and barked as though someone were stealing the horses, which was an old trick of hers. Last she returned, and her snuffing yelp said, 'I'll be good! Let me in and I'll be good!'

She was admitted and flew to her pillow. When she was quieted I whispered to the other dog, 'You can lie on the foot of the bed.' The bull jumped up at once, and though I felt Vixen quiver with rage, she knew better than to protest. So we slept till the morning, and they had early breakfast with me, bite for bite, till the horse came round and we went for a ride. I don't think the bull had ever followed a horse before. He was wild with excitement, and Vixen, as usual, squealed and scuttered and scooted, and took charge of the procession.

There was one corner of a village near by, which we generally passed with caution, because all the yellow pariah dogs of the place gathered about it. They were half-wild, starving beasts, and though utter cowards, yet where nine or ten of them get together they will mob and kill and eat an

English dog. I kept a whip with a long lash for them. That morning they attacked Vixen, who, perhaps of design, had moved from beyond my horse's shadow.

The bull was ploughing along in the dust, fifty yards behind, rolling in his run, and smiling as bull terriers will. I heard Vixen squeal; half a dozen of the curs closed in on her; a white streak came up behind me; a cloud of dust rose near Vixen, and, when it cleared, I saw one tall pariah with his back broken, and the bull wrenching another to earth. Vixen retreated to the protection of my whip, and the bull paddled back smiling more than ever, covered with the blood of his enemies. That decided me to call him 'Garm of the Bloody Breast', who was a great person in his time, or 'Garm' for short; so, leaning forward, I told him what his temporary name would be. He looked up while I repeated it, and then raced away. I shouted 'Garm!' He stopped, raced back, and came up to ask my will.

Then I saw that my soldier friend was right, and that that dog knew and was worth more than a man. At the end of the ride I gave an order which Vixen knew and hated: 'Go away and get washed!' I said. Garm understood some part of it, and Vixen interpreted the rest, and the two trotted off together soberly. When I went to the back veranda Vixen had been washed snowy-white, and was very proud of herself, but the dog-boy would not touch Garm on any account unless I stood by. So I waited while he was being scrubbed, and Garm, with the soap creaming on the top of his broad head, looked at me to make sure that this was what I expected him to endure. He knew perfectly that the dog-boy was only obeying orders.

'Another time,' I said to the dog-boy, 'you will wash the great dog with Vixen when I send them home.'

'Does *he* know?' said the dog-boy, who understood the ways of dogs.

'Garm,' I said, 'another time you will be washed with Vixen.'

14

I knew that Garm understood. Indeed, next washing-day, when Vixen as usual fled under my bed, Garm stared at the doubtful dog-boy in the veranda, stalked to the place where he had been washed last time, and stood rigid in the tub.

But the long days in my office tried him sorely. We three would drive off in the morning at half past eight and come home at six or later. Vixen, knowing the routine of it, went to sleep under my table; but the confinement ate into Garm's soul. He generally sat on the veranda looking out on the Mall; and well I knew what he expected.

Sometimes a company of soldiers would move along on their way to the Fort, and Garm rolled forth to inspect them; or an officer in uniform entered into the office, and it was pitiful to see poor Garm's welcome to the cloth – not the man. He would leap at him, and sniff and bark joyously, then run to the door and back again. One afternoon I heard him bay with a full throat – a thing I had never heard before – and he disappeared. When I drove into my garden at the end of the day a soldier in white uniform scrambled over the wall at the far end, and the Garm that met me was a joyous dog. This happened twice or thrice a week for a month.

I pretended not to notice, but Garm knew and Vixen knew. He would glide homewards from the office about four o'clock, as though he were only going to look at the scenery, and this he did so quietly that but for Vixen I should not have noticed him. The jealous little dog under the table would give a sniff and a snort, just loud enough to call my attention to the flight. Garm might go out forty times in the day and Vixen would never stir, but when he slunk off to see his true master in my garden she told me in her own tongue. That was the one sign she made to prove that Garm did not altogether belong to the family. They were the best of friends at all times, *but*, Vixen explained that I was never to forget Garm did not love me as she loved me.

I never expected it. The dog was not my dog – could never be my dog – and I knew he was as miserable as his master who tramped eight miles a day to see him. So it seemed to me that the sooner the two were reunited the better for all. One afternoon I sent Vixen home alone in the dog cart (Garm had gone before), and rode over to cantonments to find another friend of mine, who was an Irish soldier and a great friend of the dog's master.

I explained the whole case, and wound up with:

'And now Stanley's in my garden crying over his dog. Why doesn't he take him back? They're both unhappy.'

'Unhappy! There's no sense in the little man any more. But 'tis his fit.'

'What *is* his fit? He travels fifty miles a week to see the brute, and he pretends not to notice me when he sees me on the road; and I'm as unhappy as he is. Make him take the dog back.'

'It's his penance he's set himself. I told him by way av a joke, afther you'd run over him so convenient that night, whin he was dhrunk – I said if he was a Catholic he'd do penance. Off he went wid that fit in his little head *an'* a dose av fever, an' nothin' would suit but givin' you the dog as a hostage.'

'Hostage for what? I don't want hostages from Stanley.'

'For his good behaviour. He's keepin' straight now, the way it's no pleasure to associate wid him.'

'Has he taken the pledge?'

'If 'twas only that I need not care. Ye can take the pledge for three months on an' off. He sez he'll never see the dog again, an' *so*, mark you, he'll keep straight for evermore. Ye know his fits? Well, this is wan of them. How's the dog takin' it?'

'Like a man. He's the best dog in India. Can't you make Stanley take him back?'

'I can do no more than I have done. But ye know his fits. He's just doin' his penance. What will he do when he goes to the Hills? The docthor's put him on the list.'

It is the custom in India to send a certain number of invalids from each regiment up to stations in the Himalayas for the hot weather; and though the men ought to enjoy the cool and the comfort, they miss the society of the barracks down below, and do their best to come back or to avoid going. I felt that this move would bring matters to a head so I left Terence hopefully, though he called after me – 'He won't take the dog, sorr. You can lay your month's pay on that. Ye know his fits.'

I never pretended to understand Private Ortheris; and so I did the next best thing – I left him alone.

That summer the invalids of the regiment to which my friend belonged were ordered off to the Hills early, because the doctors thought marching in the cool of the day would do them good. Their route lay south to a place called Umballa, a hundred and twenty miles or more. Then they would turn east and march up into the hills to Kasauli or Dugshai or Subathoo. I dined with the officers the night before they left – they were marching at five in the morning. It was midnight when I drove into my garden and surprised a white figure flying over the wall.

'That man,' said my butler, 'has been here since nine, making talk to that dog. He is quite mad. I did not tell him to go away because he has been here many times before, and because the dog-boy told me that if I told him to go away, that great dog would immediately slay me. He did not wish to speak to the Protector of the Poor, and he did not ask for anything to eat or drink.'

'Kadir Buksh,' said I, 'that was well done, for the dog would surely have killed thee. But I do not think the white soldier will come any more.'

Garm slept ill that night and whimpered in his dreams. Once he sprang up with a clear, ringing bark, and I heard him wag his tail till it waked him and the bark died out in a howl. He had dreamed he was with his master again, and I nearly cried. It was all Stanley's silly fault.

The first halt which the detachment of invalids made was some miles from their barracks, on the Amritsar road, and ten miles distant from my house. By a mere chance one of the officers drove back for another good dinner at the Club (cooking on the line of march is always bad), and there I met him. He was a particular friend of mine, and I knew that he knew how to love a dog properly. His pet was a big fat retriever who was going up to the Hills for his health, and, though it was still April, the round, brown brute puffed and panted in the Club veranda as though he would burst.

'It's amazing,' said the officer, 'what excuses these invalids of mine make to get back to barracks. There's a man in my company now asked me for leave to go back to cantonments to pay a debt he'd forgotten. I was so taken by the idea I let him go, and he jingled off in an *ekka* as pleased as Punch. Ten miles to pay a debt! Wonder what it was really?'

'If you'll drive me home I think I can show you,' I said.

So we went over to my house in his dog cart with the retriever; and on the way I told him the story of Garm.

'I was wondering where that brute had gone to. He's the best dog in the regiment,' said my friend. 'I offered the little fellow twenty rupees for him a month ago. But he's a hostage, you say, for Stanley's good conduct. Stanley's one of the best men I have – when he chooses.'

'That's the reason why,' I said. 'A second-rate man wouldn't have taken things to heart as he has done.'

We drove in quietly at the far end of the garden, and crept round the house. There was a place close to the wall all grown about with tamarisk trees, where I knew Garm kept his bones. Even Vixen was not allowed to sit near it. In the full Indian moonlight I could see a white uniform bending over the dog.

'Goodbye, old man,' we could not help hearing Stanley's voice. 'For 'Eving's sake don't get bit and go mad by any measly pi-dog. But you can look after yourself, old man. *You* don't get drunk an' run about 'ittin' your friends. You takes your bones an' you eats your biscuit, an' you kills your enemy like a gentleman. I'm goin' away – don't 'owl – I'm goin' off to Kasauli where I won't see you no more.'

I could hear him holding Garm's nose as the dog threw it up to the stars.

'You'll stay here an' be'ave, an' – an' I'll go away an' try to be'ave, an' I don't know 'ow to leave you. I don't know –'

'I think this is damn silly,' said the officer, patting his foolish fubsy old retriever. He called to the private, who leaped to his feet, marched forward, and saluted.

'You here?' said the officer, turning away his head.

'Yes, sir, but I'm just goin' back.'

'I shall be leaving here at eleven in my cart. You come with me. I can't have sick men running about all over the place. Report yourself at eleven, *here.*'

We did not say much when we went indoors, but the officer muttered and pulled his retriever's ears.

He was a disgraceful, overfed doormat of a dog; and when he waddled off to my cookhouse to be fed, I had a brilliant idea.

At eleven o'clock that officer's dog was nowhere to be found, and you never heard such a fuss as his owner made. He called and shouted and grew angry and hunted through my garden for half an hour.

Then I said:

'He's sure to turn up in the morning. Send a man in by rail and I'll find the beast and return him.'

'Beast?' said the officer. 'I value that dog considerably more than I value any man I know. It's all very fine for you to talk – your dog's here.'

So she was – under my feet – and, had she been missing, food and wages would have stopped in my house till her return. But some people grow fond of dogs not worth a cut of the whip. My friend had to drive away at last with Stanley in the back seat; and then the dog-boy said to me:

'What kind of animal is Bullen Sahib's dog? Look at him!'

I went to the boy's hut, and the fat old reprobate was lying on a mat carefully chained up. He must have heard his master calling for twenty minutes, but had not even attempted to join him.

'He has no face,' said the dog-boy scornfully. 'He is a *punniar-kooter* (a spaniel). He never tried to get that cloth off his jaws when his master called. Now Vixen-baba would have jumped through the window, and that Great Dog would have slain me with his muzzled mouth. It is true that there are many kinds of dogs.'

Next evening who should turn up but Stanley. The officer had sent him back fourteen miles by rail with a note begging me to return the retriever if I had found him, and, if I had not, to offer huge rewards. The last train to camp left at half past ten, and Stanley stayed till ten talking to Garm. I argued and entreated, and even threatened to shoot the bull terrier, but the little man was as firm as a rock, though I gave him a good dinner and talked to him most severely. Garm knew as well as I that this was the last time he could hope to see his man, and followed Stanley like a shadow. The retriever said nothing, but licked his lips after his meal and waddled off without so much as saying 'Thank you' to the disgusted dog-boy.

So that last meeting was over and I felt as wretched as Garm, who moaned in his sleep all night. When we went to the office he found a place under the table close to Vixen, and dropped flat till it was time to go home. There was no more running out into the verandas, no slinking away for stolen talks with Stanley. As the weather grew warmer the dogs were forbidden to run beside the cart, but sat at my side on the seat, Vixen with her head under the crook of my left elbow, and Garm hugging the left handrail.

Here Vixen was ever in great form. She had to attend to all the moving traffic, such as bullock carts that blocked the way, and camels, and led ponies; as well as to keep up her dignity when she passed low friends running in the dust. She never yapped for yapping's sake, but her shrill, high bark was known all along the Mall, and other men's terriers ki-yied in reply, and bullock drivers looked over their shoulders and gave us the road with a grin.

But Garm cared for none of these things. His big eyes were on the horizon and his terrible mouth was shut. There was another dog in the office who belonged to my chief. We called him 'Bob the Librarian', because he always imagined vain rats behind the bookshelves, and in hunting for them would drag out half the old newspaper files. Bob was a well-meaning idiot, but Garm did not encourage him. He would slide his head round the door, panting, 'Rats! Come along, Garm!' and Garm would shift one forepaw over the other, and curl himself round, leaving Bob to whine at a most uninterested back. The office was nearly as cheerful as a tomb in those days.

Once, and only once, did I see Garm at all contented with his surroundings. He had gone for an unauthorised walk with Vixen early one Sunday morning and a very young and foolish artilleryman (his battery had just moved to that part of the world) tried to steal them both. Vixen, of course, knew better than to take food from soldiers, and, besides, she had just finished her breakfast. So she trotted back with a large piece of the mutton that they issue to our troops, laid it down on my veranda, and looked up to see what I thought. I asked her where Garm was, and she ran in front of the horse to show me the way.

About a mile up the road we came across our artilleryman sitting very stiffly on the edge of a culvert with a greasy handkerchief on his knees. Garm was in front of him, looking rather pleased. When the man moved leg or hand, Garm bared his teeth in silence. A broken string hung from his collar, and the other half of it lay, all warm, in the artilleryman's still hand. He explained to me, keeping his eyes straight in front of him, that he had met this dog (he called him awful names) walking alone, and was going to take him to the Fort to be killed for a masterless pariah.

I said that Garm did not seem to me much of a pariah, but that he had better take him to the Fort if he thought best. He said he did not care to do so. I told him to go to the Fort alone.

He said he did not want to go at that hour, but would follow my advice as soon as I had called off the dog. I instructed Garm to take him to the Fort, and Garm marched him solemnly up to the gate, one mile and a half under a hot sun, and I told the quarter-guard what had happened; but the young artilleryman was more angry than was at all necessary when they began to laugh. Several regiments, he was told, had tried to steal Garm in their time.

That month the hot weather shut down in earnest, and the dogs slept in the bathroom on the cool wet bricks where the bath is placed. Every morning, as soon as the man filled my bath, the two jumped in, and every morning the man filled the bath a second time. I said to him that he might as well fill a small tub specially for the dogs. 'Nay,' said he smiling, 'it is not their custom. They would not understand. Besides, the big bath gives them more space.'

The punkah-coolies who pull the punkahs day and night came to know Garm intimately. He noticed that when the swaying fan stopped I would call out to the coolie and bid him pull with a long stroke. If the man still slept I would wake him up. He discovered, too, that it was a good thing to lie in the wave of air under the punkah. Maybe Stanley had taught him all about this in barracks. At any rate, when the punkah stopped, Garm would first growl and cock his eye at the rope, and if that did not wake the man – it nearly always did – he would tiptoe forth and talk in the sleeper's ear. Vixen was a clever little dog, but she could never connect the punkah and the coolie; so Garm gave me grateful hours of cool sleep. But he was utterly wretched – as miserable as a human being; and in his misery he clung so closely to me that other men noticed it, and were envious. If I moved from one room to another, Garm followed; if my pen stopped scratching, Garm's head was thrust into my hand; if I turned, half awake, on the pillow, Garm was up and at my side, for he knew that I was his only link with his master, and day and night, and night and day, his eyes asked one question – 'When is this going to end?'

Living with the dog as I did, I never noticed that he was more than ordinarily upset by the hot weather, till one day at the Club a man said: 'That dog of yours will die in a week or two. He's a shadow.' Then I dosed Garm with iron and quinine, which he hated; and I felt very anxious. He lost his appetite, and Vixen was allowed to eat his dinner under his eyes. Even that did not make him swallow, and we held a consultation on him, of the best man doctor in the place; a lady doctor, who cured the sick wives of kings; and the Deputy Inspector General of the veterinary service of all India. They pronounced upon his symptoms, and I told them his story, and Garm lay on a sofa licking my hand.

'He's dying of a broken heart,' said the lady doctor suddenly.

''Pon my word,' said the Deputy Inspector General, 'I believe Mrs Macrae is perfectly right – as usual.'

The best man doctor in the place wrote a prescription, and the veterinary Deputy Inspector General went over it afterwards to be sure that the drugs were in the proper dog proportions; and that was the first time in his life that our doctor ever allowed his prescriptions to be edited. It was a strong tonic, and it put the dear boy on his feet for a week or two; then he lost flesh again. I asked a man I knew to take him up to the Hills with him when he went, and the man came to the door with his kit packed on the top of the carriage. Garm took in the situation at one red glance. The hair rose along his back; he sat down in front of me and delivered the most awful growl I have ever heard in the jaws of a dog. I shouted to my friend to get away at once, and as soon as the carriage was out of the garden Garm laid his head on my knee and whined. So I knew his answer, and devoted myself to getting Stanley's address in the Hills.

My turn to go to the cool came late in August. We were allowed thirty days' holiday in a year, if no one fell sick, and we took it as we could be spared. My chief and Bob the Librarian had their holiday first, and when they were gone I made a calendar, as I always did, and hung it up at the head of my cot, tearing off one day at a time till they returned. Vixen had gone up to the Hills with me five times before; and she appreciated the cold and the damp and the beautiful wood fires there as much as I did.

'Garm,' I said, 'we are going back to Stanley at Kasauli. Kasauli-Stanley; Stanley-Kasauli.' And I repeated it twenty times. It was not Kasauli really, but another place. Still I remembered what Stanley had said in my garden on the last night, and I dared not change the name. Then Garm began to tremble; then he barked; and then he leaped up at me, frisking and wagging his tail.

'Not now,' I said, holding up my hand. 'When I say "Go", we'll go, Garm.' I pulled out the little blanket coat and spiked collar that Vixen always wore up in the Hills, to protect her against sudden chills and thieving leopards, and I let the two smell them and talk it over. What they said of course I do not know, but it made a new dog of Garm. His eyes were bright; and he barked joyfully when I spoke to him. He ate his food, and he killed his rats for the next three weeks, and when he began to whine I had only to say 'Stanley-Kasauli; Kasauli-Stanley,' to wake him up. I wish I had thought of it before.

My chief came back, all brown with living in the open air, and very angry at finding it so hot in the Plains. That same afternoon we three and Kadir Buksh began to pack for our month's holiday, Vixen rolling in and out of the bullock trunk twenty times a minute, and Garm grinning all over and thumping on the floor with his tail. Vixen knew the routine of travelling as well as she knew my office work. She went to the station, singing songs, on the front seat of the carriage, while Garm sat with me. She hurried into the railway carriage, saw Kadir Buksh make up my bed for the night, got her drink of water, and curled up with her black-patch eye on the tumult of the platform. Garm followed her (the crowd gave him a lane all to himself) and sat down on the pillows with his eyes blazing, and his tail a haze behind him.

We came to Umballa in the hot misty dawn, four or five men, who had been working hard for eleven months, shouting for our dâks – the two-horse travelling carriages that were to take us up to Kalka at the foot of the Hills. It was all new to Garm. He did not understand carriages where you lay at full length on your bedding, but Vixen knew and hopped into her place at once; Garm following. The Kalka Road, before the railway was built, was about forty-seven miles long, and the horses were changed every eight miles. Most of them jibbed, and kicked, and plunged, but they had to go, and they went rather better than usual for Garm's deep bay in their rear.

There was a river to be forded, and four bullocks pulled the carriage, and Vixen stuck her head out of the sliding door and nearly fell into the water while she gave directions. Garm was silent and curious, and rather needed reassuring about Stanley and Kasauli. So we rolled, barking and yelping, into Kalka for lunch, and Garm ate enough for two.

After Kalka the road wound among the hills, and we took a curricle with half-broken ponies, which were changed every six miles. No one dreamed of a railroad to Simla in those days, for it was seven thousand feet up in the air. The road was more than fifty miles long, and the regulation pace was just as fast as the ponies could go. Here, again, Vixen led Garm from one carriage to the other; jumped into the back seat, and shouted. A cool breath from the snows met us about five miles out of Kalka, and she whined for her coat, wisely fearing a chill on the liver. I had had one made for Garm too, and, as we climbed to the fresh breezes, I put it on, and Garm chewed it uncomprehendingly, but I think he was grateful.

'Hi-yi-yi-yi!' sang Vixen as we shot round the curves; 'Toot-toot-toot!' went the driver's bugle at the dangerous places, and 'Yow! yow! yow!' bayed Garm. Kadir Buksh sat on the front seat and smiled. Even he was glad to get away from the heat of the Plains that stewed in the haze behind us. Now and then we would meet a man we knew going down to his work again, and he would shout: 'Hotter than cinders. What's it like up above?' and he would shout back: 'Just perfect!' and away we would go.

Suddenly Kadir Buksh said, over his shoulder: 'Here is Solon'; and Garm snored where he lay with his head on my knee. Solon is an unpleasant little cantonment, but it has the advantage of being cool and healthy. It is all bare and windy, and one generally stops at a rest house near by for something to eat. I got out and took both dogs with me, while Kadir Buksh made tea. A soldier told us we should find Stanley 'out there', nodding his head towards a bare, bleak hill.

When we climbed to the top we spied that very Stanley, who had given me all this trouble, sitting on a rock with his face in his hands and his overcoat hanging loose about him. I never saw anything so lonely and dejected in my life as this one little man, crumpled up and thinking, on the great grey hillside.

Here Garm left me.

He departed without a word, and, so far as I could see, without moving his legs. He flew through the air bodily, and I heard the whack of him as he flung himself at Stanley, knocking the little man clean over. They rolled on the ground together, shouting, and yelping, and hugging. I could not see which was dog and which was man, till Stanley got up and whimpered.

He told me that he had been suffering from fever at intervals, and was very weak. He looked all he said, but even while I watched, both man and dog plumped out to their natural sizes, precisely as dried apples swell in water. Garm was on his shoulder, and his breast and feet all at the same time, so that Stanley spoke all through a cloud of Garm – gulping, sobbing, slavering Garm. He did not say anything that I could understand, except that he had fancied he was going to die, but that now he was quite well, and that he was not going to give up Garm any more to anybody under the rank of Beelzebub.

Then he said he felt hungry, and thirsty, and happy.

We went down to tea at the rest house, where Stanley stuffed himself with sardines and raspberry jam, and beer, and cold mutton and pickles, when Garm wasn't climbing over him; and then Vixen and I went on.

Garm saw how it was at once. He said goodbye to me three times, giving me both paws one after another, and leaping on to my shoulder. He further escorted us, singing Hosannas at the top of his voice, a mile down the road. Then he raced back to his own master.

Vixen never opened her mouth, but when the cold twilight came, and we could see the lights of Simla across the hills, she snuffled with her nose at the breast of my ulster. I unbuttoned it, and tucked her inside. Then she gave a contented little sniff, and fell fast asleep, her head on my breast, till we bundled out at Simla, two of the four happiest people in all the world that night.

THE POWER OF THE DOG

There is sorrow enough in the natural way
From men and women to fill our day;
And when we are certain of sorrow in store,
Why do we always arrange for more?
Brothers and sisters, I bid you beware
Of giving your heart to a dog to tear.

Buy a pup and your money will buy
Love unflinching that cannot lie –
Perfect passion and worship fed
By a kick in the ribs or a pat on the head.
Nevertheless it is hardly fair
To risk your heart for a dog to tear.

When the fourteen years which Nature permits
Are closing in asthma, or tumour, or fits,
And the vet's unspoken prescription runs
To lethal chambers or loaded guns,
Then you will find – it's your own affair –
But...you've given your heart to a dog to tear.

When the body that lived at your single will,
With its whimper of welcome, is stilled (how still!),
When the spirit that answered your every mood
Is gone – wherever it goes – for good,
You will discover how much you care,
And will give your heart to a dog to tear!

We've sorrow enough in the natural way,
When it comes to burying Christian clay.
Our loves are not given, but only lent,
At compound interest of cent per cent,
Though it is not always the case, I believe,
That the longer we've kept 'em, the more do we grieve;
For, when debts are payable, right or wrong,
A short-time loan is as bad as a long –
So why in – Heaven (before we are there)
Should we give our hearts to a dog to tear?

QUIQUERN

The People of the Eastern Ice, they are melting like the snow –
They beg for coffee and sugar; they go where the white men go.
The People of the Western Ice, they learn to steal and fight;
They sell their furs to the trading post: they sell their souls to
    the white.
The People of the Southern Ice, they trade with the whaler's
    crew;
Their women have many ribbons, but their tents are torn and
    few.
But the People of the Elder Ice, beyond the white man's ken –
Their spears are made of the narwhal-horn, and they are the
    last of the Men!

Translation

'He has opened his eyes. Look!'

'Put him in the skin again. He will be a strong dog. On the fourth month we will name him.'

'For whom?' said Amoraq.

Kadlu's eye rolled round the skin-lined snow house till it fell on fourteen-year-old Kotuko sitting on the sleeping bench, making a button out of walrus ivory. 'Name him for me,' said Kotuko, with a grin. 'I shall need him one day.'

Kadlu grinned back till his eyes were almost buried in the fat of his flat cheeks, and nodded to Amoraq, while the puppy's fierce mother whined to see her baby wriggling far out of reach in the little sealskin pouch hung above the warmth of the blubber-lamp. Kotuko went on with his carving, and Kadlu threw a rolled bundle of leather dog harnesses into a tiny little room that opened from one side of the house, slipped off his heavy deerskin hunting suit, put it into a whalebone net that hung above another lamp, and dropped down on the sleeping bench to whittle at a piece of frozen seal meat till Amoraq, his wife, should bring the regular dinner of boiled meat and blood-soup. He had been out since early dawn at the seal-holes, eight miles away, and had come home with three big seal. Halfway down the long, low snow passage or tunnel that led to the inner door of the house you could hear snappings and yelpings, as the dogs of his sleigh team, released from the day's work, scuffled for warm places.

When the yelpings grew too loud Kotuko lazily rolled off the sleeping bench, and picked up a whip with an eighteen-inch handle of springy whalebone, and twenty-five feet of heavy, plaited thong. He dived into the passage, where it sounded as though all the dogs were eating him alive; but that was no more than their regular grace before meals. When he crawled out at the far end, half a dozen furry heads followed him with their eyes as he went to a sort of gallows of whale jawbones, from which the dogs' meat was hung; split off the frozen stuff in big lumps with a broad-headed spear; and stood, his whip in one hand and the meat in the other. Each beast was called by name, the weakest first, and woe betide any dog that moved out of his turn; for the tapering lash would shoot out like thonged lightning, and flick away an inch or so of hair and hide. Each beast growled, snapped, choked once over his portion, and hurried back to the protection of the passage, while the boy stood upon the snow under the blazing Northern Lights and dealt out justice. The last to be served was the big black leader of the team, who kept order when the dogs were harnessed; and to him Kotuko gave a double allowance of meat as well as an extra crack of the whip.

'Ah!' said Kotuko, coiling up the lash, 'I have a little one over the lamp that will make a great many howlings. *Sarpok!* Get in!'

He crawled back over the huddled dogs, dusted the dry snow from his furs with the whalebone beater that Amoraq kept by the door, tapped the skin-lined roof of the house to shake off any icicles that might have fallen from the dome of snow above, and curled up on the bench. The dogs in the passage snored and whined in their sleep, the boy-baby in Amoraq's deep fur hood kicked and choked and gurgled, and the mother of the newly-named puppy lay at Kotuko's side, her eyes fixed on the bundle of sealskin, warm and safe above the broad yellow flame of the lamp.

And all this happened far away to the north, beyond Labrador, beyond Hudson's Strait, where the great tides heave the ice about, north of Melville Peninsula – north even of the narrow Fury and Hecla Straits – on the north shore of Baffin Land, where Bylot's Island stands above the ice of Lancaster Sound like a pudding bowl wrong side up. North of Lancaster Sound there is little we know anything about, except North Devon and Ellesmere Land; but even there live a few scattered people, next door, as it were, to the very Pole.

Kadlu was an Inuit – what you call an Esquimau – and his tribe, some thirty persons all told, belonged to the Tununirmiut – 'the country lying at the back of something'. In the maps that desolate coast is written Navy Board Inlet, but the Inuit name is best, because the country lies at the very back of everything in the world. For nine months of the year there is only ice and snow, and gale after gale, with a cold that no one can realise who has never seen the thermometer even at zero. For six months of those nine it is dark; and that is what makes it so horrible. In the three months of the summer it only freezes every other day and every night, and then the snow begins to weep off on the southerly slopes, and a few ground-willows put out their woolly buds, a tiny stonecrop or so makes believe to blossom, beaches of fine gravel and rounded stones run down to the open sea, and polished boulders and streaked rocks lift up above the granulated snow. But all that is gone in a few weeks, and the wild winter locks down again on the land; while at sea the ice tears up and down the offing, jamming and ramming, and splitting and hitting, and pounding and grounding, till it all freezes together, ten feet thick, from the land outward to deep water.

In the winter Kadlu would follow the seal to the edge of this land ice, and spear them as they came up to breathe at their blowholes. The seal must have open water to live and catch fish in, and in the deep of winter the ice would sometimes run eighty miles without a break from the nearest shore. In the spring he and his people retreated from the floes to the rocky mainland, where they put up tents of skins, and snared the sea birds, or speared the young seal basking on the beaches. Later, they would go south into Baffin Land after the reindeer, and to get their year's store of salmon from the hundreds of streams and lakes of the interior; coming back north in September or October for the musk ox hunting and the regular winter sealery. This travelling was done with dog sleighs, twenty and thirty miles a day, or sometimes down the coast in big skin 'woman-boats', when the dogs and the babies lay among the feet of the rowers, and the women sang songs as they glided from cape to cape over the glassy, cold waters. All the luxuries that the Tununirmiut knew came from the south – driftwood for sleigh-runners, rod-iron for harpoon tips, steel knives, tin kettles that cooked food much better than the old soapstone affairs, flint and steel, and even matches, as well as coloured ribbons for the women's hair, little cheap mirrors, and red cloth for the edging of deerskin dress jackets. Kadlu traded the rich, creamy, twisted narwhal-horn and musk-ox teeth (these are just as valuable as pearls) to the Southern Inuit, and they, in turn, traded with the whalers and the missionary posts of Exeter and Cumberland Sounds; and so the chain went on, till a kettle picked up by a ship's cook in the Bhendy Bazar might end its days over a blubber-lamp somewhere on the cool side of the Arctic Circle.

Kadlu, being a good hunter, was rich in iron harpoons, snow-knives, bird-darts, and all the other things that make life easy up there in the great cold; and he was the head of his tribe, or, as they say, 'the man who knows all about it by practice.' This did not give him any authority, except now and then he could advise his friends to change their hunting grounds; but Kotuko used it to domineer a little, in the lazy, fat Inuit fashion, over the other boys, when they came out at night to play ball in the moonlight, or to sing the Child's Song to the Aurora Borealis.

But at fourteen an Inuit feels himself a man, and Kotuko was tired of making snares for wildfowl and kit-foxes, and most tired of all of helping the women to chew seal- and deer-skins (that supples them as nothing else can) the long day through, while the men were out hunting. He wanted to go into the *quaggi,* the Singing-House, when the hunters gathered there for their mysteries, and the *angekok,* the sorcerer, frightened them into the most delightful fits after the lamps were put out, and you could hear the Spirit of the Reindeer stamping on the roof; and when a spear was thrust out into the open black night it came back covered with hot blood. He wanted to throw his big boots into the net with the tired air of the head of a family, and to gamble with the hunters when they dropped in of an evening and played a sort of home-made roulette with a tin pot and a nail. There were hundreds of things that he wanted to do, but the grown men laughed at him and said, 'Wait till you have been in the buckle, Kotuko. Hunting is not *all* catching.'

Now that his father had named a puppy for him things looked brighter. An Inuit does not waste a good dog on his son till the boy knows something of dog-driving; and Kotuko was more than sure that he knew more than everything.

If the puppy had not had an iron constitution he would have died from overstuffing and over-handling. Kotuko made him a tiny harness with a trace to it, and hauled him all over the house floor, shouting: 'Aua! Ja aua!' (Go to the right.) 'Choiachoi! Ja choiachoi!' (Go to the left.) 'Ohaha!' (Stop.) The puppy did not like it at all, but being fished for in this way was pure happiness beside being put to the sleigh for the first time. He just sat down on the snow, and played with the seal-hide trace that ran from his harness to the *pitu,* the big thong in the bows of the sleigh. Then the team started, and the puppy found the heavy ten-foot sleigh running up his back, and dragging him along the snow, while Kotuko laughed till the tears ran down his face. There followed days and days of the cruel whip that hisses like the wind over ice, and his companions all bit him because he did not know his work, and the harness chafed him, and he was not allowed to sleep with Kotuko any more, but had to take the coldest place in the passage. It was a sad time for the puppy.

The boy learned, too, as fast as the dog; though a dog sleigh is a heart breaking thing to manage. Each beast is harnessed, the weakest nearest to the driver, by his own separate trace, which runs under his left foreleg to the main thong, where it is fastened by a sort of button and loop which can be slipped by a turn of the wrist, thus freeing one dog at a time. This is very necessary, because young dogs often get the trace between their hind legs, where it cuts to the bone. And they one and all *will* go visiting their friends as they run, jumping in and out among the traces. Then they fight, and the result is more mixed than a wet fishing line next morning. A great deal of trouble can be avoided by scientific use of the whip. Every Inuit boy prides himself as being a master of the long lash; but it is easy to flick at a mark on the ground, and difficult to lean forward and catch a shirking dog just behind the shoulders when the sleigh is going at full speed. If you call one dog's name for 'visiting', and accidentally lash another, the two will fight it out at once, and stop all the others. Again, if you travel with a companion and begin to talk, or by yourself and sing, the dogs will halt, turn round, and sit down to hear what you have to say. Kotuko was run away from once or twice through forgetting to block the sleigh when he stopped; and he broke many lashings, and ruined a few thongs before he could be trusted with a full team of eight and the light sleigh. Then he felt himself a person of consequence, and on smooth, black ice, with a bold heart and a quick elbow, he smoked along over the levels as fast as a pack in full cry. He would go ten miles to the seal-holes, and when he was on the hunting grounds he would twitch a trace loose from the *pitu,* and free the big black leader, who was the cleverest dog in the team. As soon as the dog had scented a breathing-hole, Kotuko would reverse the sleigh, driving a couple of sawed-off antlers, that stuck up like perambulator handles from the back-rest, deep into the snow, so that the team could not get away. Then he would crawl forward inch by inch, and wait till the seal came up to breathe. Then he would stab down swiftly with his spear and running line, and presently would haul his seal up to the lip of the ice, while the black leader came up and helped to pull the carcass across the ice to the sleigh. That was the time when the harnessed dogs yelled and foamed with excitement, and Kotuko laid the long lash like a red-hot bar across all their faces, till the carcass froze stiff. Going home was the heavy work. The loaded sleigh had to be humoured among the rough ice, and the dogs sat down and looked hungrily at the seal instead of pulling. At last they would strike the well-worn sleigh road to the village, and toodle-kiyi along the ringing ice, heads down and tails up, while Kotuko struck up the 'An-gutivaun tai-na tau-na-ne taina' (The Song of the Returning Hunter), and voices hailed him from house to house under all that dim, star-litten sky.

When Kotuko the dog came to his full growth he enjoyed himself too. He fought his way up the team steadily, fight after fight, till one fine evening, over their food, he tackled the big, black leader (Kotuko the boy saw fair play), and made second dog of him, as they say. So he was promoted to the long thong of the leading dog, running five feet in advance of all the others: it was his bounden duty to stop all fighting, in harness or out of it, and he wore a collar of copper wire, very thick and heavy. On special occasions he was fed with cooked food inside the house, and sometimes was allowed to sleep on the bench with Kotuko. He was a good seal-dog, and would keep a musk ox at bay by running round him and snapping at his heels. He would even – and this for a sleigh-dog is the last proof of bravery – he would even stand up to the gaunt Arctic wolf, whom all dogs of the North, as a rule, fear beyond anything that walks the snow. He and his master – they did not count the team of ordinary dogs as company – hunted together, day after day and night after night, fur-wrapped boy and savage, long-haired, narrow-eyed, white-fanged, yellow brute. All an Inuit has to do is to get food and skins for himself and his family. The womenfolk make the skins into clothing, and occasionally help in trapping small game; but the bulk of the food – and they eat enormously – must be found by the men. If the supply fails there is no one up there to buy or borrow from. The people must die.

An Inuit does not think of these chances till he is forced to. Kadlu, Kotuko, Amoraq, and the boy-baby who kicked about in Amoraq's fur hood and chewed pieces of blubber all day, were as happy together as any family in the world. They came of a very gentle race – an Inuit seldom loses his temper, and almost never strikes a child – who did not know exactly what telling a real lie meant, still less how to steal. They were content to spear their living out of the heart of the bitter, hopeless cold; to smile oily smiles, and tell queer ghost and fairy tales of evenings, and eat till they could eat no more, and sing the endless woman's song: 'Amna aya, aya amna, ah! ah!' through the long lamp-lighted days as they mended their clothes and their hunting gear.

But one terrible winter everything betrayed them. The Tununirmiut returned from the yearly salmon fishing, and made their houses on the early ice to the north of Bylot's

Island, ready to go after the seal as soon as the sea froze. But it was an early and savage autumn. All through September there were continuous gales that broke up the smooth seal-ice when it was only four or five feet thick, and forced it inland, and piled a great barrier, some twenty miles broad, of lumped and ragged and needly ice; over which it was impossible to draw the dog sleighs. The edge of the floe off which the seal were used to fish in winter lay perhaps twenty miles beyond this barrier, and out of reach of the Tununirmiut. Even so, they might have managed to scrape through the winter on their stock of frozen salmon and stored blubber, and what the traps gave them, but in December one of their hunters came across a *tupik* (a skin-tent) of three women and a girl nearly dead, whose men had come down from the far North and been crushed in their little skin hunting boats while they were out after the long-horned narwhal. Kadlu, of course, could only distribute the women among the huts of the winter village, for no Inuit dare refuse a meal to a stranger. He never knows when his own turn may come to beg. Amoraq took the girl, who was about fourteen, into her own house as a sort of servant. From the cut of her sharp-pointed hood, and the long diamond pattern of her white deerskin leggings, they supposed she came from Ellesmere Land. She had never seen tin cooking pots or wooden-shod sleighs before; but Kotuko the boy and Kotuko the dog were rather fond of her.

Then all the foxes went south, and even the wolverine, that growling, blunt-headed little thief of the snow, did not take the trouble to follow the line of empty traps that Kotuko set. The tribe lost a couple of their best hunters, who were badly crippled in a fight with a musk ox, and this threw more work on the others. Kotuko went out, day after day, with a light hunting sleigh and six or seven of the strongest dogs, looking till his eyes ached for some patch of clear ice where a seal might perhaps have scratched a breathing-hole. Kotuko the dog ranged far and wide, and in the dead stillness of the ice fields

Kotuko the boy could hear his half-choked whine of excitement, above a seal-hole three miles away, as plainly as though he were at his elbow. When the dog found a hole the boy would build himself a little, low snow wall to keep off the worst of the bitter wind, and there he would wait ten, twelve, twenty hours for the seal to come up to breathe, his eyes glued to the tiny mark he had made above the hole to guide the downward thrust of his harpoon, a little sealskin mat under his feet, and his legs tied together in the *tutareang* (the buckle that the old hunters had talked about). This helps to keep a man's legs from twitching as he waits and waits and waits for the quick-eared seal to rise. Though there is no excitement in it, you can easily believe that the sitting still in the buckle with the thermometer perhaps forty degrees below zero is the hardest work an Inuit knows. When a seal was caught, Kotuko the dog would bound forward, his trace trailing behind him, and help to pull the body to the sleigh, where the tired and hungry dogs lay sullenly under the lee of the broken ice.

A seal did not go very far, for each mouth in the little village had a right to be filled, and neither bone, hide, nor sinew was wasted. The dogs' meat was taken for human use, and Amoraq fed the team with pieces of old summer skin-tents raked out from under the sleeping bench, and they howled and howled again, and waked to howl hungrily. One could tell by the soap-stone lamps in the huts that famine was near. In good seasons, when blubber was plentiful, the light in the boat-shaped lamps would be two feet high – cheerful, oily, and yellow. Now it was a bare six inches: Amoraq carefully pricked down the moss wick, when an unwatched flame brightened for a moment, and the eyes of all the family followed her hand. The horror of famine up there in the great cold is not so much dying, as dying in the dark. All the Inuit dread the dark that presses on them without a break for six months in each year; and when the lamps are low in the houses the minds of people begin to be shaken and confused.

But worse was to come.

The underfed dogs snapped and growled in the passages, glaring at the cold stars, and snuffing into the bitter wind, night after night. When they stopped howling the silence fell down again as solid and as heavy as a snowdrift against a door, and men could hear the beating of their blood in the thin passages of the ear, and the thumping of their own hearts, that sounded as loud as the noise of sorcerers' drums beaten across the snow. One night Kotuko the dog, who had been unusually sullen in harness, leaped up and pushed his head against Kotuko's knee. Kotuko patted him, but the dog still pushed blindly forward, fawning. Then Kadlu waked, and gripped the heavy wolflike head, and stared into the glassy eyes. The dog whimpered and shivered between Kadlu's knees. The hair rose about his neck, and he growled as though a stranger were at the door; then he barked joyously, and rolled on the ground, and bit at Kotuko's boot like a puppy.

'What is it?' said Kotuko; for he was beginning to be afraid.

'The sickness,' Kadlu answered. 'It is the dog-sickness.' Kotuko the dog lifted his nose and howled and howled again.

'I have not seen this before. What will he do?' said Kotuko.

Kadlu shrugged one shoulder a little, and crossed the hut for his short stabbing-harpoon. The big dog looked at him, howled again, and slunk away down the passage, while the other dogs drew aside right and left to give him ample room. When he was out on the snow he barked furiously, as though on the trail of a musk ox, and, barking and leaping and frisking, passed out of sight. His trouble was not hydrophobia, but simple, plain madness. The cold and the hunger, and, above all, the dark, had turned his head; and when the terrible dog-sickness once shows itself in a team, it spreads like wildfire. Next hunting day another dog sickened, and was killed then and there by Kotuko as he bit and struggled among the traces. Then the black second dog, who had been the leader in the old days, suddenly gave tongue on an imaginary reindeer track, and when they slipped him from the *pitu* he flew at the throat of an ice cliff, and ran

40

away as his leader had done, his harness on his back. After that no one would take the dogs out again. They needed them for something else, and the dogs knew it; and though they were tïed down and fed by hand, their eyes were full of despair and fear. To make things worse, the old women began to tell ghost tales, and to say that they had met the spirits of the dead hunters lost that autumn, who prophesied all sorts of horrible things.

Kotuko grieved more for the loss of his dog than anything else; for though an Inuit eats enormously he also knows how to starve. But the hunger, the darkness, the cold, and the exposure told on his strength, and he began to hear voices inside his head, and to see people who were not there, out of the tail of his eye. One night – he had unbuckled himself after ten hours' waiting above a 'blind' seal-hole, and was staggering back to the village faint and dizzy – he halted to lean his back against a boulder which happened to be supported like a rocking-stone on a single jutting point of ice. His weight disturbed the balance of the thing, it rolled over ponderously, and as Kotuko sprang aside to avoid it, slid after him, squeaking and hissing on the ice slope.

That was enough for Kotuko. He had been brought up to believe that every rock and boulder had its owner (its *inua*), who was generally a one-eyed kind of a Woman-Thing called a *tornaq*, and that when a *tornaq* meant to help a man she rolled after him inside her stone house, and asked him whether he would take her for a guardian spirit. (In summer thaws the ice-propped rocks and boulders roll and slip all over the face of the land, so you can easily see how the idea of live stones arose.) Kotuko heard the blood beating in his ears as he had heard it all day, and he thought that was the *tornaq* of the stone speaking to him. Before he reached home he was quite certain that he had held a long conversation with her, and as all his people believed that this was quite possible, no one contradicted him.

'She said to me, "I jump down, I jump down from my place on the snow," ' cried Kotuko, with hollow eyes, leaning forward in the half-lighted hut. 'She said, "I will be a guide." She says, "I will guide you to the good seal-holes." Tomorrow I go out, and the *tornaq* will guide me.'

Then the *angekok,* the village sorcerer, came in, and Kotuko told him the tale a second time. It lost nothing in the telling.

'Follow the *tornait* [the spirits of the stones], and they will bring us food again,' said the *angekok.*

Now the girl from the North had been lying near the lamp, eating very little and saying less for days past; but when Amoraq and Kadlu next morning packed and lashed a little hand sleigh for Kotuko, and loaded it with his hunting gear and as much blubber and frozen seal meat as they could spare, she took the pulling-rope, and stepped out boldly at the boy's side.

'Your house is my house,' she said, as the little bone-shod sleigh squeaked and bumped behind them in the awful Arctic night.

'My house is your house,' said Kotuko; 'but *I* think that we shall both go to Sedna together.'

Now Sedna is the Mistress of the Underworld, and the Inuit believe that every one who dies must spend a year in her horrible country before going to Quadliparmiut, the Happy Place, where it never freezes and the fat reindeer trot up when you call.

Through the village people were shouting: 'The *tornait* have spoken to Kotuko. They will show him open ice. He will bring us the seal again!' Their voices were soon swallowed up by the cold, empty dark, and Kotuko and the girl shouldered close together as they strained on the pulling-rope or humoured the sleigh through the ice in the direction of the Polar Sea. Kotuko insisted that the *tornaq* of the stone had told him to go north, and north they went under Tuktuqdjung the Reindeer – those stars that we call the Great Bear.

No European could have made five miles a day over the ice-rubbish and the sharp-edged drifts; but those two knew exactly the turn of the wrist that coaxes a sleigh round a hummock, the jerk that neatly lifts it out of an ice-crack, and the exact strength that goes to the few quiet strokes of the spearhead that make a path possible when everything looks hopeless.

The girl said nothing, but bowed her head, and the long wolverine-fur fringe of her ermine hood blew across her broad, dark face. The sky above them was an intense velvety black, changing to bands of Indian red on the horizon, where the great stars burned like street lamps. From time to time a greenish wave of the Northern Lights would roll across the hollow of the high heavens, flick like a flag, and disappear; or a meteor would crackle from darkness to darkness, trailing a shower of sparks behind. Then they could see the ridged and furrowed surface of the floe tipped and laced with strange colours – red, copper, and bluish; but in the ordinary starlight everything turned to one frost-bitten grey. The floe, as you will remember, had been battered and tormented by the autumn gales till it was one frozen earthquake. There were gullies and ravines, and holes like gravel pits cut in ice; lumps and scattered pieces frozen down to the original floor of the floe; blotches of old black ice that had been thrust under the floe in some gale and heaved up again; roundish boulders of ice; saw-like edges of ice carved by the snow that flies before the wind; and sunken pits where thirty or forty acres lay below the level of the rest of the field. From a little distance you might have taken the lumps for seal or walrus, overturned sleighs or men on a hunting expedition, or even the great Ten-legged White Spirit-Bear himself; but in spite of these fantastic shapes, all on the very edge of starting into life, there was neither sound nor the least faint echo of sound. And through this silence and through this waste, where the sudden lights flapped and went out again, the sleigh and the two that pulled it crawled like things in a nightmare – a nightmare of the end of the world at the end of the world.

When they were tired Kotuko would make what the hunters call a 'half-house', a very small snow hut, into which they would huddle with the travelling lamp, and try to thaw out the frozen seal meat. When they had slept, the march began again – thirty miles a day to get ten miles northward. The girl was always very silent, but Kotuko muttered to himself and broke out into songs he had learned in the Singing-House – summer songs, and reindeer and salmon songs – all horribly out of place at that season. He would declare that he heard the *tornaq* growling to him, and would run wildly up a hummock, tossing his arms and speaking in loud, threatening tones. To tell the truth, Kotuko was very nearly crazy for the time being; but the girl was sure that he was being guided by his guardian spirit, and that everything would come right. She was not surprised, therefore, when at the end of the fourth march Kotuko, whose eyes were burning like fireballs in his head, told her that his *tornaq* was following them across the snow in the shape of a two-headed dog. The girl looked where Kotuko pointed, and something seemed to slip into a ravine. It was certainly not human, but everybody knew that the *tornait* preferred to appear in the shape of bear and seal, and suchlike.

It might have been the Ten-legged White Spirit-Bear himself, or it might have been anything, for Kotuko and the girl were so starved that their eyes were untrustworthy. They had trapped nothing, and seen no trace of game since they had left the village; their food would not hold out for another week, and there was a gale coming. A Polar storm can blow for ten days without a break, and all that while it is certain death to be abroad. Kotuko laid up a snow house large enough to take in the hand sleigh (never be separated from your meat), and while he was shaping the last irregular block of ice that makes the keystone of the roof, he saw a Thing looking at him from a little cliff of ice half a mile away. The air was hazy, and the Thing seemed to be forty feet long and ten feet high with twenty feet of tail and a shape that quivered all along the out-lines. The girl saw it too, but instead of crying aloud with terror, said quietly, 'That is Quiquern. What comes after?'

'He will speak to me,' said Kotuko; but the snow-knife trembled in his hand as he spoke, because however much a man may believe that he is a friend of strange and ugly spirits, he seldom likes to be taken quite at his word. Quiquern, too, is the phantom of a gigantic toothless dog without any hair, who is supposed to live in the far North, and to wander about the country just before things are going to happen. They may be pleasant or unpleasant things, but not even the sorcerers care to speak about Quiquern. He makes the dogs go mad. Like the Spirit-Bear, he has several extra pairs of legs – six or eight – and this Thing jumping up and down in the haze had more legs than any real dog needed. Kotuko and the girl huddled into their hut quickly. Of course if Quiquern had wanted them, he could have torn it to pieces above their heads, but the sense of a foot-thick snow wall between themselves and the wicked dark was great comfort. The gale broke with a shriek of wind like the shriek of a train, and for three days and three nights it held, never varying one point, and never lulling even for a minute. They fed the stone lamp between their knees, and nibbled at the half-warm seal meat, and watched the black soot gather on the roof for seventy-two long hours. The girl counted up the food in the sleigh; there was not more than two days' supply, and Kotuko looked over the iron heads and the deer-sinew fastenings of his harpoon and his seal-lance and his bird-dart. There was nothing else to do.

'We shall go to Sedna soon – very soon,' the girl whispered. 'In three days we shall lie down and go. Will your *tornaq* do nothing? Sing her an *angekok's* song to make her come here.'

He began to sing in the high-pitched howl of the magic songs, and the gale went down slowly. In the middle of his song the girl started, laid her mittened hand and then her head to the ice floor of the hut. Kotuko followed her example, and the two kneeled, staring into each other's eyes, and listening with every nerve. He ripped a thin sliver of whalebone from the rim of a bird-snare that lay on the sleigh, and, after straightening, set it upright in a little bole in the ice, firming it down with his mitten. It was almost as delicately adjusted as a compass needle, and now instead of listening they watched. The thin rod quivered a little – the least little jar in the world; then it vibrated steadily for a few seconds, came to rest, and vibrated again, this time nodding to another point of the compass.

'Too soon!' said Kotuko. 'Some big floe has broken far away outside.'

The girl pointed at the rod, and shook her head. 'It is the big breaking,' she said. 'Listen to the ground ice. It knocks.'

When they kneeled this time they heard the most curious muffled grunts and knockings, apparently under their feet. Sometimes it sounded as though a blind puppy were squeaking above the lamp; then as if a stone were being ground on hard ice; and again, like muffled blows on a drum; but all dragged out and made small, as though they travelled through a little horn a weary distance away.

'We shall not go to Sedna lying down,' said Kotuko. 'It is the breaking. The *tornaq* has cheated us. We shall die.'

All this may sound absurd enough, but the two were face to face with a very real danger. The three days' gale had driven the deep water of Baffin's Bay southerly, and piled it on to the edge of the far-reaching land ice that stretches from Bylot's Island to the west. Also, the strong current which sets east out of Lancaster Sound carried with it mile upon mile of what they call pack ice – rough ice that has not frozen into fields; and this pack was bombarding the floe at the same time that the swell and heave of the storm-worked sea was weakening and under-mining it. What Kotuko and the girl had been listening to were the faint echoes of that fight thirty or forty miles away, and the little tell-tale rod quivered to the shock of it.

Now, as the Inuit say, when the ice once wakes after its long winter sleep, there is no knowing what may happen, for solid floe ice changes shape almost as quickly as a cloud. The gale was evidently a spring gale sent out of time, and anything was possible.

Yet the two were happier in their minds than before. If the floe broke up there would be no more waiting and suffering. Spirits, goblins, and witch people were moving about on the racking ice, and they might find themselves stepping into Sedna's country side by side with all sorts of wild Things, the flush of excitement still on them. When they left the hut after the gale, the noise on the horizon was steadily growing, and the tough ice moaned and buzzed all round them.

'It is still waiting,' said Kotuko.

On the top of a hummock sat or crouched the eight-legged Thing that they had seen three days before – and it howled horribly.

'Let us follow,' said the girl. 'It may know some way that does not lead to Sedna'; but she reeled from weakness as she took the pulling-rope. The Thing moved off slowly and clumsily across the ridges, heading always toward the westward and the land; and they followed, while the growling thunder at the edge of the floe rolled nearer and nearer. The floe's lip was split and cracked in every direction for three or four miles inland, and great pans of ten-foot-thick ice, from a few yards to twenty acres square, were jolting and ducking and surging into one another, and into the yet unbroken floe, as the heavy swell took and shook and spouted between them. This battering-ram ice was, so to speak, the first army that the sea was flinging against the floe. The incessant crash and jar of these cakes almost drowned the ripping sound of sheets of pack ice driven bodily under the floe as cards are hastily pushed under a tablecloth. Where the water was shallow these sheets would be piled one atop of the other till the bottommost touched mud fifty feet down, and the discoloured sea banked behind the muddy ice till the increasing pressure drove all forward again. In addition to the floe and the pack ice, the gale and the currents were bringing down true bergs, sailing mountains of ice, snapped off from the Greenland side of the water or the north shore of Melville Bay. They pounded in solemnly, the waves breaking white round them, and advanced on the floe like an old-time fleet under full sail. A berg that seemed ready to carry the world before it would ground helplessly in deep water, reel over, and wallow in a lather of foam and mud and flying frozen spray, while a much smaller and lower one would rip and ride into the flat floe, flinging tons of ice on either side, and cutting a track half a mile long before it was stopped. Some fell like swords, shearing a raw-edged canal; and others splintered into a shower of blocks, weighing scores of tons apiece, that whirled and skirled among the hummocks. Others, again, rose up bodily out of the water when they shoaled, twisted as though in pain, and fell solidly on their sides, while the sea threshed over their shoulders. This trampling and crowding and bending and buckling and arching of the ice into every possible shape was going on as far as the eye could reach all along the north line of the floe. From where Kotuko and the girl were, the confusion looked no more than an uneasy, rippling, crawling movement under the horizon; but it came toward them each moment, and they could hear, far away to landward, a heavy booming, as it might have been the boom of artillery through a fog. That showed that the floe was being jammed home against the iron cliffs of Bylot's Island, the land to the southward behind them.

'This has never been before,' said Kotuko, staring stupidly. 'This is not the time. How can the floe break *now?*'

'Follow *that!*' the girl cried, pointing to the Thing half limping, half running distractedly before them. They followed, tugging at the hand sleigh, while nearer and nearer came the roaring march of the ice. At last the fields round them cracked and starred in every direction, and the cracks opened and snapped like the teeth of wolves. But where the Thing rested, on a mound of old and scattered ice blocks some fifty feet high, there was no motion. Kotuko leaped forward wildly, dragging the girl after him, and crawled to the bottom of the mound. The talking of the ice grew louder and louder round them, but the mound stayed fast, and, as the girl looked at him, he threw his right elbow upward and outward, making the Inuit sign for land in the shape of an island. And land it was that the eight-legged, limping Thing had led them to – some granite-tipped, sand-beached islet off the coast, shod and sheathed and masked with ice so that no man could have told it from the floe, but at the bottom solid earth, and not shifting ice! The smashing and rebound of the floes as they grounded and splintered marked the borders of it, and a friendly shoal ran out to the northward, and turned aside the rush of the heaviest ice, exactly as a ploughshare turns over loam. There was danger, of course, that some heavily squeezed ice field might shoot up the beach, and plane off the top of the islet bodily; but that did not trouble Kotuko and the girl when they made their snow house and began to eat, and heard the ice hammer and skid along the beach. The Thing had disappeared, and Kotuko was talking excitedly about his power over spirits as he crouched round the lamp. In the middle of his wild sayings the girl began to laugh, and rock herself backward and forward.

Behind her shoulder, crawling into the hut crawl by crawl, there were two heads, one yellow and one black, that belonged to two of the most sorrowful and ashamed dogs that ever you saw. Kotuko the dog was one, and the black leader was the other. Both were now fat, well-looking, and quite restored to their proper minds, but coupled to each other in an extra-ordinary fashion. When the black leader ran off, you remember, his harness was still on him. He must have met Kotuko the dog, and played or fought with him, for his shoulder loop had caught in the plaited copper wire of Kotuko's collar, and had drawn tight, so that neither could get at the trace to gnaw it apart, but each was fastened sidelong to his neighbour's neck. That, with the freedom of hunting on their own account, must have helped to cure their madness. They were very sober.

The girl pushed the two shamefaced creatures towards Kotuko, and, sobbing with laughter, cried, 'That is Quiquern, who led us to safe ground. Look at his eight legs and double head!'

Kotuko cut them free, and they fell into his arms, yellow and black together, trying to explain how they had got their senses back again. Kotuko ran a hand down their ribs, which were round and well clothed. 'They have found food,' he said, with a grin. 'I do not think we shall go to Sedna so soon. My *tornaq* sent these. The sickness has left them.'

As soon as they had greeted Kotuko, these two, who had been forced to sleep and eat and hunt together for the past few weeks, flew at each other's throat, and there was a beautiful battle in the snow house. 'Empty dogs do not fight,' Kotuko said. 'They have found the seal. Let us sleep. We shall find food.'

When they waked there was open water on the north beach of the island, and all the loosened ice had been driven landward. The first sound of the surf is one of the most delightful that the Inuit can hear, for it means that spring is on the road. Kotuko and the girl took hold of hands and smiled, for the clear, full roar of the surge among the ice reminded them of salmon and reindeer time and the smell of blossoming ground-willows. Even as they looked, the sea began to skim over between the floating cakes of ice, so intense was the cold; but on the horizon there was a vast red glare, and that was the light of the sunken sun. It was more like hearing him yawn in his sleep than seeing him rise and the glare lasted for only a few minutes, but it marked the turn of the year. Nothing, they felt, could alter that.

Kotuko found the dogs fighting over a fresh-killed seal who was following the fish that a gale always disturbs. He was the first of some twenty or thirty seal that landed on the island in the course of the day, and till the sea froze hard there were hundreds of keen black heads rejoicing in the shallow free water and floating about with the floating ice.

It was good to eat seal liver again; to fill the lamps recklessly with blubber, and watch the flame blaze three feet in the air; but as soon as the new sea ice bore, Kotuko and the girl loaded the hand sleigh, and made the two dogs pull as they had never pulled in their lives, for they feared what might have happened in their village. The weather was as pitiless as usual; but it is easier to draw a sleigh loaded with good food than to hunt starving. They left five-and-twenty seal carcasses buried in the ice of the beach, all ready for use, and hurried back to their people. The dogs showed them the way as soon as Kotuko told them what was expected, and though there was no sign of a landmark, in two days they were giving tongue outside Kadlu's house. Only three dogs answered them; the others had been eaten, and the houses were all dark. But when Kotuko shouted, 'Ojo!' (boiled meat), weak voices replied, and when he called the muster of the village name by name, very distinctly, there were no gaps in it.

An hour later the lamps blazed in Kadlu's house; snow water was heating; the pots were beginning to simmer, and the snow was dripping from the roof as Amoraq made ready a meal for all the village, and the boy-baby in the hood chewed at a strip of rich nutty blubber, and the hunters slowly and methodically filled themselves to the very brim with seal meat. Kotuko and the girl told their tale. The two dogs sat between them, and whenever their names came in, they cocked an ear apiece and looked most thoroughly ashamed of themselves. A dog who has once gone mad and recovered, the Inuit say, is safe against all further attacks.

'So the *tornaq* did not forget us,' said Kotuko. 'The storm blew, the ice broke, and the seal swam in behind the fish that were frightened by the storm. Now the new seal-holes are not two days distant. Let the good hunters go tomorrow and bring back the seal I have speared – twenty-five seal buried in the ice. When we have eaten those we will all follow the seal on the floe.'

'What do *you* do?' said the sorcerer in the same sort of voice as he used to Kadlu, richest of the Tununirmiut.

Kadlu looked at the girl from the North, and said quietly, '*We* build a house.' He pointed to the north-west side of Kadlu's house, for that is the side on which the married son or daughter always lives.

The girl turned her hands palm upward, with a little despairing shake of her head. She was a foreigner, picked up starving, and could bring nothing to the housekeeping.

Amoraq jumped from the bench where she sat, and began to sweep things into the girl's lap – stone lamps, iron skin-scrapers, tin kettles, deerskins embroidered with musk-ox teeth, and real canvas needles such as sailors use – the finest dowry that has ever been given on the far edge of the Arctic Circle, and the girl from the North bowed her head down to the very floor.

'Also these!' said Kotuko, laughing and signing to the dogs, who thrust their cold muzzles into the girl's face.

'Ah,' said the *angekok,* with an important cough, as though he had been thinking it all over. 'As soon as Kotuko left the village I went to the Singing-House and sang magic. I sang all the long nights, and called upon the Spirit of the Reindeer. *My* singing made the gale blow that broke the ice and drew the two dogs toward Kotuko when the ice would have crushed his bones. *My* song drew the seal in behind the broken ice. My body lay still in the *quaggi,* but my spirit ran about on the ice, and guided Kotuko and the dogs in all the things they did. I did it.'

Everybody was full and sleepy, so no one contradicted; and the *angekok,* by virtue of his office, helped himself to yet another lump of boiled meat, and lay down to sleep with the others in the warm, well-lighted, oil-smelling home.

Now Kotuko, who drew very well in the Inuit fashion, scratched pictures of all these adventures on a long, flat piece of ivory with a hole at one end. When he and the girl went north to Ellesmere Land in the year of the Wonderful Open Winter, he left the picture story with Kadlu, who lost it in the shingle when his dog sleigh broke down one summer on the beach of Lake Netilling at Nikosiring, and there a Lake Inuit found it next spring and sold it to a man at Imigen who was interpreter on a Cumberland Sound whaler, and he sold it to Hans Olsen, who was afterward a quartermaster on board a big steamer that took tourists to the North Cape in Norway. When the tourist season was over, the steamer ran between London and Australia, stopping at Ceylon, and there Olsen sold the ivory to a Cingalese jeweller for two imitation sapphires. I found it under some rubbish in a house at Colombo, and have translated it from one end to the other.

THE DOG HERVEY

My friend Attley, who would give away his own head if you told him you had lost yours, was giving away a six-months-old litter of Bettina's pups, and half a dozen women were in raptures at the show on Mittleham lawn.

We picked by lot. Mrs Godfrey drew first choice; her married daughter, second. I was third, but waived my right because I was already owned by Malachi, Bettina's full brother, whom I had brought over in the car to visit his nephews and nieces, and he would have slain them all if I had taken home one. Milly, Mrs Godfrey's younger daughter, pounced on my rejection with squeals of delight, and Attley turned to a dark, sallow-skinned, slack-mouthed girl, who had come over for tennis, and invited her to pick. She put on a pair of pince-nez that made her look like a camel, knelt clumsily, for she was long from the hip to the knee, breathed hard, and considered the last couple.

'I think I'd like that sandy-pied one,' she said.

'Oh, not him, Miss Sichliffe!' Attley cried. 'He was overlaid or had sunstroke or something. They call him The Looney in the kennels. Besides, he squints.'

'I think that's rather fetching,' she answered. Neither Malachi nor I had ever seen a squinting dog before.

'That's chorea – St Vitus' dance,' Mrs Godfrey put in. 'He ought to have been drowned.'

'But I like his cast of countenance,' the girl persisted.

'He doesn't look a good life,' I said, 'but perhaps he can be patched up.' Miss Sichliffe turned crimson; I saw Mrs Godfrey exchange a glance with her married daughter, and knew I had said something which would have to be lived down.

'Yes,' Miss Sichliffe went on, her voice shaking, 'he isn't a good life, but perhaps I can – patch him up. Come here, sir.' The misshapen beast lurched toward her, squinting down his own nose till he fell over his own toes. Then, luckily, Bettina ran across the lawn and reminded Malachi of their puppyhood. All that family are as queer as Dick's hatband, and fight like man and wife. I had to separate them, and Mrs Godfrey helped me till they retired under the rhododendrons and had it out in silence.

'D'you know what that girl's father was?' Mrs Godfrey asked.

'No,' I replied. 'I loathe her for her own sake. She breathes through her mouth.'

'He was a retired doctor,' she explained. 'He used to pick up stormy young men in the repentant stage, take them home, and patch them up till they were sound enough to be insured. Then he insured them heavily, and let them out into the world again – with an appetite. Of course, no one knew him while he was alive, but he left pots of money to his daughter.'

'Strictly legitimate – highly respectable,' I said. 'But what a life for the daughter!'

'Mustn't it have been! *Now* d'you realise what you said just now?'

'Perfectly; and now you've made me quite happy, shall we go back to the house?'

When we reached it they were all inside, sitting on committee of names.

'What shall you call yours?' I heard Milly ask Miss Sichliffe.

'Harvey,' she replied – 'Harvey's Sauce, you know. He's going to be quite saucy when I've' – she saw Mrs Godfrey and me coming through the French window – 'when he's stronger.'

Attley, the well-meaning man, to make me feel at ease, asked what I thought of the name.

'Oh, splendid,' I said at random. 'H with an A, A with an R, R with a –'

'But that's Little Bingo,' someone said, and they all laughed.

Miss Sichliffe, her hands joined across her long knees, drawled, 'You ought always to verify your quotations.'

It was not a kindly thrust, but something in the word 'quotation' set the automatic side of my brain at work on some shadow of a word or phrase that kept itself out of memory's reach as a cat sits just beyond a dog's jump. When I was going home, Miss Sichliffe came up to me in the twilight, the pup on a leash, swinging her big shoes at the end of her tennis racket.

"Sorry,' she said in her thick schoolboy-like voice. 'I'm sorry for what I said to you about verifying quotations. I didn't know you well enough and – anyhow, I oughtn't to have.'

'But you were quite right about Little Bingo,' I answered. 'The spelling ought to have reminded me.'

'Yes, of course. It's the spelling,' she said, and slouched off with the pup sliding after her. Once again my brain began to worry after something that would have meant something if it had been properly spelled. I confided my trouble to Malachi on the way home, but Bettina had bitten him in four places, and he was busy.

Weeks later, Attley came over to see me, and before his car stopped Malachi let me know that Bettina was sitting beside the chauffeur. He greeted her by the scruff of the neck as she hopped down; and I greeted Mrs Godfrey, Attley, and a big basket.

'You've got to help me,' said Attley tiredly. We took the basket into the garden, and there staggered out the angular shadow of a sandy-pied, broken-haired terrier, with one imbecile and one delirious ear, and two most hideous squints. Bettina and Malachi, already at grips on the lawn, saw him, let go, and fled in opposite directions.

56

'Why have you brought that fetid hound here?' I demanded.

'Harvey? For you to take care of,' said Attley. 'He's had distemper, but *I'm* going abroad.'

'Take him with you. I won't have him. He's mentally afflicted.'

'Look here,' Attley almost shouted, 'do I strike you as a fool?'

'Always,' said I.

'Well, then, if you say so, and Ella says so, that proves I ought to go abroad.'

'Will's wrong, quite wrong,' Mrs Godfrey interrupted; 'but you must take the pup.'

'My dear boy, my dear boy, don't you ever give anything to a woman,' Attley snorted.

Bit by bit I got the story out of them in the quiet garden (never a sign from Bettina and Malachi), while Harvey stared me out of countenance, first with one cuttlefish eye and then with the other.

It appeared that, a month after Miss Sichliffe took him, the dog Harvey developed distemper. Miss Sichliffe had nursed him herself for some time; then she carried him in her arms the two miles to Mittleham, and wept – actually wept – at Attley's feet, saying that Harvey was all she had or expected to have in this world, and Attley must cure him. Attley, being by wealth, position, and temperament guardian to all lame dogs, had put everything aside for this unsavoury job, and, he asserted, Miss Sichliffe had virtually lived with him ever since.

'She went home at night, of course,' he exploded, 'but the rest of the time she simply infested the premises. Goodness knows, I'm not particular, but it was a scandal. Even the servants!... Three and four times a day, and notes in between, to know how the beast was. Hang it all, don't laugh! And wanting to send me flowers and goldfish. Do I look as if I wanted goldfish? Can't you two stop for a minute?' (Mrs Godfrey and I were clinging to each other for support.) 'And it isn't as if I was – was so alluring a personality, is it?'

Attley commands more trust, goodwill, and affection than most men, for he is that rare angel, an absolutely unselfish bachelor, happy to be run by contending syndicates of zealous friends. His situation seemed desperate, and I told him so.

'Instant flight is your only remedy,' was my verdict. 'I'll take care of both your cars while you're away, and you can send me over all the greenhouse fruit.'

'But why should I be chased out of my house by a she-dromedary?' he wailed.

'Oh, stop! Stop!' Mrs Godfrey sobbed. 'You're both wrong. I admit you're right, but I *know* you're wrong.'

'Three *and* four times a day,' said Attley, with an awful countenance. 'I'm not a vain man, but – look here, Ella, I'm not sensitive, I hope, but if you persist in making a joke of it – '

'Oh, be quiet!' she almost shrieked. 'D'you imagine for one instant that your friends would ever – let Mittleham pass out of their hands? I quite agree it is unseemly for a grown girl to come to Mittleham at all hours of the day and night – '

'I told you she went home o' nights,' Attley growled.

'Specially if she goes home o' nights. Oh, but think of the life she must have led, Will!'

'I'm not interfering with it; only she must leave me alone.'

'She may want to patch you up and insure you,' I suggested.

'D'you know what *you* are?' Mrs Godfrey turned on me with the smile I have feared for the last quarter of a century. 'You're the nice, kind, wise, doggy friend. You don't know how wise and nice you are supposed to be. Will has sent Harvey to you to complete the poor angel's convalescence. You know all about dogs, or Will wouldn't have done it. He's written her that. You're too far off for her to make daily calls on you. P'r'aps she'll drop in two or three times a week, and write on other days. But it doesn't matter what she does, because you don't own Mittleham, don't you see?'

I told her I saw most clearly.

58

'Oh, you'll get over that in a few days,' Mrs Godfrey countered. 'You're the sporting, responsible, doggy friend who – '

'He used to look at me like that at first,' said Attley, with a visible shudder, 'but he gave it up after a bit. It's only because you're new to him.'

'But confound you! He's a ghoul – ' I began.

'And when he gets quite well, you'll send him back to her direct with your love, and she'll give you some pretty four-tailed goldfish,' said Mrs Godfrey, rising. 'That's all settled. Car, please. We're going to Brighton to lunch together.'

They ran before I could get into my stride, so I told the dog Harvey what I thought of them and his mistress. He never shifted his position, but stared at me, an intense, lopsided stare, eye after eye. Malachi came along when he had seen his sister off and from a distance counselled me to drown the brute and consort with gentlemen again. But the dog Harvey never even cocked his cockable ear.

And so it continued as long as he was with me. Where I sat, he sat and stared; where I walked, he walked beside, head stiffly slewed over one shoulder in single-barrelled contemplation of me. He never gave tongue, never closed in for a caress, seldom let me stir a step alone. And, to my amazement, Malachi, who suffered no stranger to live within our gates, saw this gaunt, growing, green-eyed devil wipe him out of my service and company without a whimper. Indeed, one would have said the situation interested him, for he would meet us returning from grim walks together, and look alternately at Harvey and at me with the same quivering interest that he showed at the mouth of a rat hole. Outside these inspections, Malachi withdrew himself as only a dog or a woman can.

Miss Sichliffe came over after a few days (luckily I was out) with some elaborate story of paying calls in the neighbourhood. She sent me a note of thanks next day. I was reading it when Harvey and Malachi entered and disposed themselves as usual, Harvey close up to stare at me, Malachi half under the sofa, watching us both. Out of curiosity I returned Harvey's stare, then pulled his lopsided head on to my knee, and took his eye for several minutes. Now, in Malachi's eye I can see at any hour all that there is of the normal decent dog, flecked here and there with that strained half-soul which man's love and association have added to his nature. But with Harvey perplexed, as a tortured man's. Only by looking far into its deeps could one make out the spirit of the proper animal, beclouded and cowering beneath some unfair burden.

Leggatt, my chauffeur, came in for orders.

'How d'you think Harvey's coming on?' I said, as I rubbed the brute's gulping neck. The vet had warned me of the possibilities of spinal trouble following distemper.

'He ain't *my* fancy,' was the reply. 'But *I* don't question his comings and goings so long as I 'aven't to sit alone in a room with him.'

'Why? He's as meek as Moses,' I said.

'He fair gives me the creeps. P'r'aps he'll go out in fits.'

But Harvey, as I wrote his mistress from time to time, throve, and when he grew better, would play by himself grisly games of spying, walking up, hailing, and chasing another dog. From these he would break off of a sudden and return to his normal stiff gait, with the air of one who had forgotten some matter of life and death, which could be reached only by staring at me. I left him one evening posturing with the unseen on the lawn, and went inside to finish some letters for the post. I must have been at work nearly an hour, for I was going to turn on the lights, when I felt there was somebody in the room whom, the short hairs at the back of my neck warned me, I was not in the least anxious to face. There was a mirror on the wall. As I lifted my eyes to it I saw the dog Harvey reflected near the shadow by the closed door. He had reared himself full-length on his hind legs, his head a little one side to clear a sofa between us, and he was looking at me. The face, with its knitted brows and drawn lips, was the face of a dog, but the look, for the fraction of time that I caught it, was human – wholly and horribly human. When the blood in my body went forward again he had dropped to the floor, and was merely studying me in his usual one-eyed fashion. Next day I returned him to Miss Sichliffe. I would not have kept him another day for the wealth of Asia, or even Ella Godfrey's approval.

Miss Sichliffe's house I discovered to be a mid-Victorian mansion of peculiar villainy even for its period, surrounded by gardens of conflicting colours, all dazzling with glass and fresh paint on ironwork. Striped blinds, for it was a blazing autumn morning, covered most of the windows, and a voice sang to the piano an almost forgotten song of Jean Ingelow's –

> Methought that the stars were blinking bright,
>   And the old brig's sails unfurled –

Down came the loud pedal, and the unrestrained cry swelled out across a bed of tritomas consuming in their own fires –

> When I said I will sail to my love this night
>   On the other side of the world.

I have no music, but the voice drew. I waited till the end:

> Oh, maid most dear, I am not here;
>   I have no place apart –
> No dwelling more on sea or shore,
>   But only in thy heart.

It seemed to me a poor life that had no more than that to do at eleven o'clock of a Tuesday forenoon. Then Miss Sichliffe suddenly lumbered through a French window in clumsy haste, her brows contracted against the light.

'Well?' she said, delivering the word like a spear-thrust, with the full weight of a body behind it.

'I've brought Harvey back at last,' I replied. 'Here he is.'

But it was at me she looked, not at the dog who had cast himself at her feet – looked as though she would have fished my soul out of my breast on the instant.

'Wha – what did you think of him? What did *you* make of him?' she panted. I was too taken aback for the moment to reply. Her voice broke as she stooped to the dog at her knees. 'O Harvey, Harvey! You utterly worthless old devil!' she cried, and the dog cringed and abased himself in servility that one could scarcely bear to look upon. I made to go.

'Oh, but please, you mustn't!' She tugged at the car's side. 'Wouldn't you like some flowers or some orchids? We've really splendid orchids, and' – she clasped her hands – 'there are Japanese goldfish – real Japanese goldfish, with four tails. If you don't care for 'em, perhaps your friends or somebody – oh, please!'

Harvey had recovered himself; and I realised that this woman beyond the decencies was fawning on me as the dog had fawned on her.

'Certainly,' I said, ashamed to meet her eye. 'I'm lunching at Mittleham, but – '

'There's plenty of time,' she entreated. 'What do *you* think of Harvey?'

'He's a queer beast,' I said, getting out. 'He does nothing but stare at me.'

'Does he stare at you all the time he's with you?'

'Always. He's doing it now. Look!'

We had halted. Harvey had sat down, and was staring from one to the other with a weaving motion of the head.

'He'll do that all day,' I said. 'What is it, Harvey?'

'Yes, what *is* it, Harvey?' she echoed. The dog's throat twitched, his body stiffened and shook as though he were going to have a fit. Then he came back with a visible wrench to his unwinking watch.

'Always so?' she whispered.

'Always,' I replied, and told her something of his life with me. She nodded once or twice, and in the end led me into the house.

There were unaging pitch-pine doors of Gothic design in it; there were inlaid marble mantelpieces and cut-steel fenders; there were stupendous wallpapers, and octagonal, medallioned Wedgwood whatnots, and black-and-gilt Austrian images holding candelabra, with every other refinement that Art had achieved or wealth had bought between 1851 and 1878. And everything reeked of varnish.

'Now!' she opened a baize door, and pointed down a long corridor flanked with more Gothic doors. 'This was where we used to – to patch 'em up. You've heard of us. Mrs Godfrey told you in the garden the day I got Harvey given me. I' – she drew in her breath – 'I live here by myself and I have a very large income. Come back, Harvey.'

He had tiptoed down the corridor, as rigid as ever, and was sitting outside one of the shut doors. 'Look here!' she said, and planted herself squarely in front of me. 'I tell you this because you – you've patched up Harvey, too. Now, I want you to remember that my name is Moira. Mother calls me Marjorie because it's more refined; but my real name is Moira, and I am in my thirty-fourth year.'

'Very good,' I said. 'I'll remember all that.'

'Thank you.' Then with a sudden swoop into the humility of an abashed boy – 'Sorry if I haven't said the proper things. You see – there's Harvey looking at us again. Oh, I want to say – if ever you want anything in the way of orchids or goldfish or – or anything else that would be useful to you, you've only to come to me for it. Under the will I'm perfectly independent, and we're a long-lived family, worse luck!' She looked at me, and her face worked like glass behind driven flame. 'I may reasonably expect to live another fifty years,' she said.

'Thank you, Miss Sichliffe,' I replied. 'If I want anything, you may be sure I'll come to you for it.' She nodded. 'Now I must get over to Mittleham,' I said.

'Mr Attley will ask you all about this.' For the first time she laughed aloud. 'I'm afraid I frightened him nearly out of the county. I didn't think, of course. But I dare say he knows by this time he was wrong. Say goodbye to Harvey.'

'Goodbye, old man,' I said. 'Give me a farewell stare, so we shall know each other when we meet again.'

The dog looked up, then moved slowly toward me, and stood, head bowed to the floor, shaking in every muscle as I patted him; and when I turned, I saw him crawl back to her feet.

That was not a good preparation for the rampant boy-and-girl-dominated lunch at Mittleham, which, as usual, I found in possession of everybody except the owner.

'But what did the dromedary say when you brought her beast back?' Attley demanded.

'The usual polite things,' I replied. 'I'm posing as the nice doggy friend nowadays.'

'I don't envy you. She's never darkened my doors, thank goodness, since I left Harvey at your place. I suppose she'll run about the county now swearing you cured him. That's a woman's idea of gratitude.' Attley seemed rather hurt and Mrs Godfrey laughed.

'That proves you were right about Miss Sichliffe, Ella,' I said. 'She had no designs on anybody.'

'I'm always right in these matters. But didn't she even offer you a goldfish?'

'Not a thing,' said I. 'You know what an old maid's like where her precious dog's concerned.' And though I have tried vainly to lie to Ella Godfrey for many years, I believe that in this case I succeeded.

When I turned into our drive that evening, Leggatt observed half aloud:

'I'm glad Svengali's back where he belongs. It's time our Mike had a look in.'

Sure enough, there was Malachi back again in spirit as well as flesh, but still with that odd air of expectation he had picked up from Harvey.

It was in January that Attley wrote me that Mrs Godfrey, wintering in Madeira with Milly, her unmarried daughter, had been attacked with something like enteric; that the hotel, anxious for its good name, had thrust them both out into a cottage annexe; that he was off with a nurse, and that I was not to leave England till I heard from him again. In a week he wired that Milly was down as well, and that I must bring out two more nurses, with suitable delicacies.

Within seventeen hours I had got them all aboard the Cape boat, and had seen the women safely collapsed into seasickness. The next few weeks were for me, as for the invalids, a low delirium, clouded with fantastic memories of Portuguese officials trying to tax calves'-foot jelly; voluble doctors insisting that true typhoid was unknown in the island; nurses who had to be exercised, taken out of themselves, and returned on the tick of change of guard; night slides down glassy, cobbled streets, smelling of sewage and flowers, between walls whose every stone and patch Attley and I knew; vigils in stucco verandas, watching the curve and descent of great stars or drawing auguries from the break of dawn; insane interludes of gambling at the local Casino, where we won heaps of unconsoling silver; blasts of steamers arriving and departing in the roads; help offered by total strangers, grabbed at or thrust aside; the long nightmare crumbling back into sanity one forenoon under a vine-covered trellis, where Attley sat hugging a nurse, while the others danced a noiseless, neat-footed breakdown never learned at the Middlesex Hospital. At last, as the tension came out all over us in aches and tingles that we put down to the country wine, a vision of Mrs Godfrey, her grey hair turned to spun glass, but her eyes triumphant over the shadow of retreating death beneath them, with Milly, enormously grown, and clutching life back to her young breast, both stretched out on cane chairs, clamouring for food.

In this ungirt hour there imported himself into our life a youngish-looking middle-aged man of the name of Shend, with a blurred face and deprecating eyes. He said he had gambled with me at the Casino, which was no recommendation, and I remember that he twice gave me a basket of champagne and liqueur brandy for the invalids, which a sailor in a red-tasselled cap carried up to the cottage for me at 3 a.m. He turned out to be the son of some merchant prince in the oil and colour line, and the owner of a four-hundred-ton steam yacht, into which, at his gentle insistence, we later shifted our camp, staff, and equipage, Milly weeping with delight to escape from the horrible cottage. There we lay off Funchal for weeks, while Shend did miracles of luxury and attendance through deputies, and never once asked how his guests were enjoying themselves. Indeed, for several days at a time we would see nothing of him. He was, he said, subject to malaria. Giving as they do with both hands, I knew that Attley and Mrs Godfrey could take nobly; but I never met a man who so nobly gave and so nobly received thanks as Shend did.

'Tell us why you have been so unbelievably kind to us gypsies,' Mrs Godfrey said to him one day on deck.

He looked up from a diagram of some Thames-mouth shoals, which he was explaining to me, and answered with his gentle smile:

'I will. It's because it makes me happy – it makes me more than happy to be with you. It makes me comfortable. You know how selfish men are? If a man feels comfortable all over with certain people, he'll bore them to death, just like a dog. You always make me feel as if pleasant things were going to happen to me.

'Haven't any ever happened before?' Milly asked.

'This is the most pleasant thing that has happened to me in ever so many years,' he replied. 'I feel like the man in the Bible, "It's good for me to be here." Generally, I don't feel that it's good for me to be anywhere in particular.' Then, as one begging a favour: 'You'll let me come home with you – in the same boat, I mean? I'd take you back in this thing of mine, and that would save you packing your trunks, but she's too lively for spring work across the Bay.'

We booked our berths, and when the time came, he wafted us and ours aboard the Southampton mailboat with the pomp of plenipotentiaries and the precision of the Navy. Then he dismissed his yacht, and became an inconspicuous passenger in a cabin opposite to mine, on the port side.

We ran at once into early British spring weather, followed by sou'west gales. Mrs Godfrey, Milly, and the nurses disappeared. Attley stood it out, visibly yellowing, till the next meal, and followed suit, and Shend and I had the little table all to ourselves. I found him even more attractive when the women were away. The natural sweetness of the man, his voice, and bearing all fascinated me, and his knowledge of practical seamanship (he held an extra master's certificate) was a real joy. We sat long in the empty saloon and longer in the smoking-room, making dashes downstairs over slippery decks at the eleventh hour.

It was on Friday night, just as I was going to bed, that he came into my cabin, after cleaning his teeth, which he did half a dozen times a day.

'I say,' he began hurriedly, 'do you mind if I come in here for a little? I'm a bit edgy.' I must have shown surprise. 'I'm ever so much better about liquor than I used to be, but – it's the whisky in the suitcase that throws me. For God's sake, old man, don't go back on me tonight! Look at my hands!'

They were fairly jumping at the wrists. He sat down on a trunk that had slid out with the roll. We had reduced speed, and were surging in confused seas that pounded on the black port glasses. The night promised to be a pleasant one!

'You understand, of course, don't you?' he chattered.

'Oh yes,' I said cheerily; 'but how about –'

'No, no; on no account the doctor. Tell a doctor, tell the whole ship. Besides, I've only got a touch of 'em. You'd never have guessed it, would you? The tooth-wash does the trick. I'll give you the prescription.'

'I'll send a note to the doctor for a prescription, shall I?' I suggested.

'Right! I put myself unreservedly in your hands. Fact is, I always did, I said to myself – sure I don't bore you? – the minute I saw you, I said, "Thou art the man."' He repeated the phrase as he picked at his knees. 'All the same, you can take it from me that the ewe-lamb business is a rotten bad one. I don't care how unfaithful the shepherd may be. Drunk or sober, 'tisn't cricket.'

A surge of the trunk threw him across the cabin as the steward answered my bell. I wrote my requisition to the doctor while Shend was struggling to his feet.

'What's wrong?' he began. 'Oh, I know. We're slowing for soundings off Ushant. It's about time, too. You'd better ship the deadlights when you come back, Matchem. It'll save you waking us later. This sea's going to get up when the tide turns. That'll show you,' he said as the man left, 'that I am to be trusted. You – you'll stop me if I say anything I shouldn't, won't you?'

'Talk away,' I replied, 'if it makes you feel better.'

'That's it; you've hit it exactly. You always make me feel better. I can rely on you. It's awkward soundings, but you'll see me through it. We'll defeat him yet... I may be an utterly worthless devil, but I'm not a brawler... I told him so at break-fast. I said, "Doctor, I detest brawling, but if ever you allow that girl to be insulted again as Clements insulted her, I will break your neck with my own hands." You think I was right?'

'Absolutely,' I agreed.

'Then we needn't discuss the matter any further. That man was a murderer in intention – outside the law, you understand, as it was then. They've changed it since – but he never deceived *me*. I told him so. I said to him at the time, "I don't know what price you're going to put on my head, but if ever you allow Clements to insult her again, you'll never live to claim it." '

'And what did he do?' I asked, to carry on the conversation, for Matchem entered with the bromide.

'Oh, crumpled up at once. Lead still going, Matchem?'

'I 'aven't 'eard,' said that faithful servant of the Union-Castle Company.

'Quite right. Never alarm the passengers. Ship the deadlight, will you?' Matchem shipped it, for we were rolling very heavily. There were tramplings and gull-like cries from on deck. Shend looked at me with a mariner's eye.

'That's nothing,' he said protectingly.

'Oh, it's all right for you,' I said, jumping at the idea. '*I* haven't an extra master's certificate. I'm only a passenger. I confess it funks me.'

Instantly his whole bearing changed to answer the appeal.

'My dear fellow, it's as simple as houses. We're hunting for sixty-five-fathom water. Anything short of sixty, with a sou'-west wind means – but I'll get my Channel Pilot out of my cabin and give you the general idea. I'm only too grateful to do anything to put your mind at ease.'

And so, perhaps, for another hour – he declined to drink – Channel Pilot in hand, he navigated us round Ushant, and at my request up-Channel to Southampton, light by light, with explanations and reminiscences. I professed myself soothed at last, and suggested bed.

'In a second,' said he. 'Now, you wouldn't think, would you' – he glanced off the book toward my wildly swaying dressing gown on the door – 'that I've been seeing things for the last half-hour? Fact is, I'm just on the edge of 'em, skating on thin ice round the corner – nor'east as near as nothing – where that dog's looking at me.'

'What's the dog like?' I asked.

'Ah, that *is* comforting of you! Most men walk through 'em to show me they aren't real. As if I didn't know! But *you*'re different. Anybody could see that with half an eye.' He stiffened and pointed. 'Damn it all! The dog sees it too with half an – Why, he knows you! Knows you perfectly. D'you know *him?*'

'How can I tell if he isn't real?' I insisted.

'But you can! *You*'re all right. I saw that from the first. Don't go back on me now or I shall go to pieces like the *Drummond Castle*. I beg your pardon, old man; but, you see, you *do* know the dog. I'll prove it. What's that dog doing? Come on! *You* know.' A tremor shook him, and he put his hand on my knee, and whispered with great meaning: 'I'll letter or halve it with you. There! You begin.'

'S,' said I to humour him, for a dog would most likely be standing or sitting, or may be scratching or sniffing or staring.

'Q,' he went on, and I could feel the heat of his shaking hand.

'U,' said I. There was no other letter possible; but I was shaking too.

'I.'

'N.'

'T-i-n-g,' he ran out. 'There! That proves it. I knew you knew him. You don't know what a relief that is. Between ourselves, old man, he – he's been turning up lately a – a damn sight more often than I cared for. And a squinting dog – a dog that squints! I mean that's a bit *too* much. Eh? What?' He gulped and half rose, and I thought that the full tide of delirium would be on him in another sentence.

'Not a bit of it,' I said as a last chance, with my hand over the bellpush. 'Why, you've proved that I know him; so there are two of us in the game, anyhow.'

70

'By Jove! That *is* an idea! Of course there are. I knew you'd see me through. We'll defeat them yet. Hi, pup!... He's gone. Absolutely disappeared!' He sighed with relief, and I caught the lucky moment.

'Good business! I expect he only came to have a look at me,' I said. 'Now, get this drink down and turn in to the lower bunk.'

He obeyed, protesting that he could not inconvenience me, and in the midst of apologies sank into a dead sleep. I expected a wakeful night, having a certain amount to think over; but no sooner had I scrambled into the top bunk than sleep came on me like a wave from the other side of the world.

In the morning there were apologies, which we got over at breakfast before our party were about.

'I suppose – after this – well, I don't blame you. I'm rather a lonely chap, though.' His eyes lifted doglike across the table.

'Shend,' I replied, 'I'm not running a Sunday School. You're coming home with me in my car as soon as we land.'

'That is kind of you – kinder than you think.'

'That's because you're a little jumpy still. Now, I don't want to mix up in your private affairs – '

'But I'd like you to,' he interrupted.

'Then, would you mind telling me the Christian name of a girl who was insulted by a man called Clements?'

'Moira,' he whispered; and just then Mrs Godfrey and Milly came to table with their shore-going hats on.

We did not tie up till noon, but the faithful Leggatt had intrigued his way down to the dock edge, and beside him sat Malachi, wearing his collar of gold, or Leggatt makes it look so, as eloquent as Demosthenes. Shend flinched a little when he saw him. We packed Mrs Godfrey and Milly into Attley's car – they were going with him to Mittleham, of course – and drew clear across the railway lines to find England all lit and perfumed for spring. Shend sighed with happiness.

'D'you know,' he said, 'if – if you'd chucked me – I should have gone down to my cabin after breakfast and cut my throat. And now – it's like a dream – a good dream, you know.'

We lunched with the other three at Romsey. Then I sat in front for a little while to talk to my Malachi. When I looked back, Shend was solidly asleep, and stayed so for the next two hours, while Leggatt chased Attley's fat Daimler along the green-speckled hedges. He woke up when we said goodbye at Mittleham, with promises to meet again very soon.

'And I hope,' said Mrs Godfrey, 'that everything pleasant will happen to you.

'Heaps and heaps – all at once,' cried long, weak Milly, waving her wet handkerchief.

'I've just got to look in at a house near here for a minute to inquire about a dog,' I said, 'and then we will go home.'

'I used to know this part of the world,' he replied, and said no more till Leggatt shot past the lodge at the Sichliffes' gate. Then I heard him gasp.

Miss Sichliffe, in a green waterproof, an orange jersey, and a pinkish leather hat, was working on a bulb border. She straightened herself as the car stopped, and breathed hard. Shend got out and walked towards her. They shook hands, turned round together, and went into the house. Then the dog Harvey pranced out corkily from under the lee of a bench. Malachi, with one joyous swoop, fell on him as an enemy and an equal. Harvey, for his part, freed from all burden whatsoever except the obvious duty of a man-dog on his own ground, met Malachi without reserve or remorse, and with six months' additional growth to come and go on.

'Don't check 'em!' cried Leggatt, dancing round the flurry. 'They've both been saving up for each other all this time. It'll do 'em worlds of good.'

'Leggatt,' I said, 'will you take Mr Shend's bag and suitcase up to the house and put them down just inside the door? Then we will go on.'

So I enjoyed the finish alone. It was a dead heat, and they licked each other's jaws in amity till Harvey, one imploring eye on me, leaped into the front seat, and Malachi backed his appeal. It was theft, but I took him, and we talked all the way home of r-rats and r-rabbits and bones and baths and the other basic facts of life. That evening after dinner they slept before the fire, with their warm chins across the hollows of my ankles – to each chin an ankle – till I kicked them upstairs to bed.

I was not at Mittleham when she came over to announce her engagement, but I heard of it when Mrs Godfrey and Attley came, forty miles an hour, over to me, and Mrs Godfrey called me names of the worst for suppression of information.

'As long as it wasn't me, I don't care,' said Attley.

'I believe you knew it all along,' Mrs Godfrey repeated. 'Else what made you drive that man literally into her arms?'

'To ask after the dog Harvey,' I replied.

'Then, what's the beast doing here?' Attley demanded, for Malachi and the dog Harvey were deep in a council of the family with Bettina, who was being out-argued.

'Oh, Harvey seemed to think himself *de trop* where he was,' I said. 'And she hasn't sent after him. You'd better save Bettina before they kill her.'

'There's been enough lying about that dog,' said Mrs Godfrey to me. 'If he wasn't born in lies, he was baptised in 'em. D'you know why she called him Harvey? It only occurred to me in those dreadful days when I was ill, and one can't keep from thinking, and thinks everything. D'you know your Boswell? What did Johnson say about Hervey – with an e?'

'Oh, *that's* it, is it?' I cried incautiously. 'That was why I ought to have verified my quotations. The spelling defeated me. Wait a moment, and it will come back. Johnson said: "He was a vicious man," ' I began.

' "But very kind to me," ' Mrs Godfrey prompted. Then, both together, ' "If you call a dog Hervey, I shall love him." '

'So you *were* mixed up in it. At any rate, you had your suspicions from the first? Tell me,' she said.

'Ella,' I said, 'I don't know anything rational or reasonable about any of it. It was all – all woman-work, and it scared me horribly.'

'Why?' she asked.

That was six years ago. I have written this tale to let her know – wherever she may be.

THE WOMAN IN HIS LIFE

DINAH IN HEAVEN

She did not know that she was dead,
    But, when the pang was o'er,
Sat down to wait her Master's tread
    Upon the Golden Floor

With ears full-cock and anxious eyes,
    Impatiently resigned;
But ignorant that Paradise
    Did not admit her kind.

Persons with Haloes, Harps, and Wings
    Assembled and reproved,
Or talked to her of Heavenly things,
    But Dinah never moved.

There was one step along the Stair
    That led to Heaven's Gate;
And, till she heard it, her affair
    Was – she explained – to wait.

And she explained with flattened ear,
    Bared lip and milky tooth –
Storming against Ithuriel's Spear
    That only proved her truth!

Sudden – far down the Bridge of Ghosts
   That anxious spirits clomb –
She caught that step in all the hosts,
   And knew that he had come.

She left them wondering what to do,
   But not a doubt had she.
Swifter than her own squeals she flew
   Across the Glassy Sea;

Flushing the Cherubs everywhere,
   And skidding as she ran,
She refuged under Peter's Chair
   And waited for her man.

There spoke a Spirit out of the press,
   Said: – 'Have you any here
That saved a fool from drunkenness,
   And a coward from his fear?

'That turned a soul from dark to day
   When other help was vain?
That snatched it from wanhope and made
   A cur a man again?'

'Enter and look,' said Peter then,
   And set The Gate ajar.
'If I know aught of women and men
   I trow she is not far.'

'Neither by virtue, speech nor art
   Nor hope of grace to win;
But godless innocence of heart
   That never heard of sin:

'Neither by beauty nor belief
  Nor white example shown.
Something a wanton – more a thief;
  But – most of all – mine own.'

'Enter and look,' said Peter then,
  'And send you well to speed;
But, for all that I know of women and men,
  Your riddle is hard to read.'

Then flew Dinah from under the Chair,
  Into his arms she flew –
And licked his face from chin to hair
  And Peter passed them through!

THE WOMAN IN HIS LIFE

Fairest of darkie daughters
Was Dinah Doe!

Negro Melody

From his boyhood John Marden had a genius for improvising or improving small labour-saving gadgets about his father's house and premises. So, when the War came, shortly after he had been apprenticed to a tool-making firm in the Midlands, he chose the Engineers, and eventually found himself at a place called Messines, where he worked underground, many months, among interesting devices. There he met a Cockney named Burnea, who diagnosed sick machinery by touch – with his eyes shut. Between them, and a few fellow workers, Messines Ridge went up.

After the War, the two men joined forces on four thousand pounds capital; a dozen young veterans of Messines; a lease of some sheds in a London suburb, and a collection of second-hand lathes and stampers. They gave out that they were ready to make anything for anybody.

A South African mine manager asked about a detachable arrangement on a drill-head, which he could not buy in open market for less than four shillings and seven pence wholesale. Marden considered the drawings, cut down the moving parts a half; Burnea made an astonished machine undertake strange duties, and by the time he had racked it to bits, they were delivering the article at one shilling and ten pence. A newly opened mine on a crest of the Andes, where llamas were, for the moment, cheaper than lorries, needed metal stiffenings and clips for pack saddles (drawing enclosed). The first model went back in a month. In another fortnight the order was filled, with improvements. At the end of their first year, an Orinoco dredging concern, worried over some barges which did not handle auriferous sludge as they ought; and a wildcat proposition on a New Guinea beach where natives treated detonating capsules with contempt; were writing their friends that you could send Burnea and Marden the roughest sketches of what you wanted, because they understood them.

So the firm flourished. The young veterans drove the shifts ten hours a day; the versatile but demoralised machinery was displaced by sterner stuff; and their third year's profits ran into five figures. Then Burnea, who had the financial head, died of pulmonary trouble, a by-product of gas-poison, and left Marden his share of the Works, plus thirty-six thousand pounds all on fixed deposit in a Bank, because the head of one of its branches had once been friendly with him in a trench. The Works were promptly enlarged, and Marden worked fourteen hours a day instead of twelve, and, to save time, followed Burnea's habit of pushing money which he did not need into the same Bank at the same meek rate of interest. But, for the look of the thing, he hired a genuine financial secretary, who was violently affected when John explained the firm's theory of investments, and recommended some alterations, which Marden was too busy to attend to. Six months later, there fell on him three big contracts, which surpassed his dreams of avarice. At this point he took what sleep was forced on him in a cot in Burnea's old office. At this point, too, Jerry Floyd, ex-Sergeant of Sappers at Messines, and drawing eighteen pounds a week with irregular bonuses, struck loudly.

'What's the matter with your job, Jerry?' John asked.

"'Tain't a job – that's all. My machines do everything for me except strike. *I've* got to do that,' said Jerry with reproach.

'Soft job. Stick to it,' John counselled.

'Stick to bloomin' what? Turnin' two taps and fiddlin' three levers? Get a girl to do it for you. Repetition work! I'm fed up!'

'Take ten days' leave, you fool,' said John; which Jerry did, and was arrested for exceeding the speed limit through angry gypsies at Brough horse fair. John Marden went to bed behind his office as usual, and – without warning – suffered a night so memorable that he looked up the nearest doctor in the Directory, and went to see him. Being inarticulate, except where the Works were concerned, he explained that he felt as though he had got the hump – was stale, fed up, and so forth. He thought, perhaps, he might have been working a bit too hard; but he said not a word of the horror, the blackness, the loss of the meaning of things, the collapses at the end, the recovery and retraversing of the circle of that night's Inferno; nor how it had waked up a certain secret dread which he had held off him since demobilisation.

'Can't you rest a bit?' asked the doctor, whose real interests were renal calculi.

'I've never tried.'

'Haven't you any hobbies or – friends, then?'

'Except the Works, none.'

'Nothing – more important in your life?'

John's face was answer enough. 'No! No! But what'll I do? What'll I *do?*' he asked wildly. 'I – I have never been like this before!'

'I'll give you a sedative, but you must slack off, and divert your mind. Yes! That's it. Divert your mind.'

John went back to the Works, and strove to tell his secretary something about the verdict. The man was perfunctorily sympathetic, but what he wanted John to understand (he seemed at the other end of the world as he spoke) was that, owing to John's ignorance of finance, the whole of the Works stood as

John's personal property. So that, if John died, they would be valued and taxed thirty or forty per cent for death duties, and that would cripple things badly. Not a minute should be lost before turning the concern into a chain of companies. He had the scheme drafted. It would need but a couple of days' study. John looked at the papers, listened to the explanations, stared at a calendar on the wall, and heard himself speaking as from the bottom of a black, cold crater:

'It don't mean anything – half a million or three quarters or – or – or anything. Oh, sorry! It's gone up like the Ridge, and I'm a dud, you know.'

Then he returned to his expensive flat, which the same secretary had taken for him a year before, and prepared to do nothing for a month except to think upon the night he had passed in Burnea's old office, and to expect, and get, others like it. A few men came – once each – grinned at him, told him to buck up, and went on to their own concerns. He was ministered to by his ex-batman, Corporal Vincent Shingle, systematically a peculator, intermittently a drunkard, and emphatically a liar. Twice – once underground, where he had penetrated with a thermos full of hot coffee, and a piece of gallery had sat down on him; and once at Bailleul, when the lunatics of the local asylum were let out, and he was chased by a homicidal maniac with a thigh bone – Marden had saved Shingle's life. Twice – once out of the crumbling rim of a crater; and once by the slack of his breeches, when a whiff of gas dropped him over the mouth of a shaft – he had saved Marden's. Therefore, he came along with the rest of the Messines veterans to the Works, whence Jerry Floyd kicked him into space at the end of the first month. Upon this, he returned to John Marden's personal service and the study of John's private correspondence and more intimate possessions. As he explained to Probert, the janitor of the flats, the night after the doctor had spoken:

'The 'ole game of gettin' on is to save your bloke trouble. 'E don't know it, but I do 'is 'omework for 'im while 'e makes money for me at 'is office. Na-ow! 'E don't spend it on me. *That* I 'ave to do meself. But I don't grudge the labour.'

'Then what's 'e been seein' the doctor *about?*' said Probert, who had an impure mind.

''Cause 'e's got what Jerry Floyd 'ad. 'E's fed up with re-petition work and richness. I've watched it comin' on. It's the same as we used to 'ave it in the War – but t'other way round. You can't mistake.'

'What's goin' to 'appen?'

'Gawd knows! I'm standin' to. The doctor 'as told 'im to lie off everythin' for a month – in one motion. If you stop runnin' machinery without slowin' 'er down, she'll lift 'erself off the bedplate. I've seen so with pumps.'

But machinery suddenly arrested has no resources in itself. Human mechanism under strain finds comfort in a drink or two. Running about in cars with no definite object bored John Marden as much as drumming beneath the clouds in aeroplanes; theatres made him think impotently of new gadgets for handling the scenery, or extracting opera glasses from their clips; cards and golf ended in his counting the pips in his hand, or the paces between shot and shot; whereas drinks softened the outlines of things, if not at once, then after a little repetition work.

The result came when a Fear leaped out of the goose-fleshed streets of London between the icy shop fronts, and drove John to his flat. He argued that it must have been a chill, and fortified himself against it so resolutely that an advertisement, which had caught the tail-end of his eye, stood up before him in the shape of a full-sized red-and-white bullock, dancing in a teacup. It was succeeded a few days later by a small dog, pressed against the skirting board of his room – an inky, fat horror with a pink tongue, crouched in the attitude of a little beast he had often watched at Mr Willham's fashionable West End pet shop, where dogs lived in excelsior-floored cubicles, appealing to the passers-by. It began as a spreading blur, which morning after morning became more definite. It was better than the ox in the teacup, till it was borne in on John Marden one dawn that, if It crawled out into the centre of the room, the Universe would crash down on him. He wondered till he sweated, dried and broke out again, what would happen to him then, and how suicides were judged. After a drink or two, he became cunning and diplomatic with – of all experts in the world – his batman, to whom he told the tale of a friend who 'saw things'. The result was tabulated that afternoon in the basement, where Shingle and Probert were drinking his whisky.

'Well – now we're arrivin' at objective A,' said Shingle. 'I knew last week 'e'd begun seein' 'em, 'cause 'e couldn't turn 'is eyes out o' corners. O' course, 'e says it's overtook a friend of 'is.'

'Reasonable enough,' said Probert. 'We all keep that friend.'

'Let's get down to figures,' Shingle went on. 'Two bottles is 'is week's whack. *An'* we know 'e don't use cocktails. Well; that don't make much more'n four drinks a day. You can't get nothin' special on that issue – not in nature.'

'Women *also?'* Probert suggested.

'Be-e damned! I know there ain't. No. It's a black dawg. That's neither 'ere nor there. But, if it comes out into the room, 'is pore friend'll go off 'is rocker. That is objective B.'

'Ye-es,' said Probert. 'I've 'ad 'em too. What about it?'

'I'm askin' you if reel dawgs are allowed in the flats. Are they?' said Shingle.

Probert dismissed the matter loftily.

'As between *us!'* he began. 'Don't stay awake for it! I've sanctioned kittens in two flats this spring. What's the game?'

''Air o' the dog that bit 'im,' Shingle answered. 'I mean 'is pore friend!'

'What about small arms in 'is possession,' said Probert. '*You* know.'

'On'y 'is pistol, an' 'e'll 'ave a proper 'unt for that. Now mind you don't go back on what you said about keepin' dawgs 'ere.'

Shingle went off, dressed in most items out of his master's wardrobe, with the pawn ticket for his master's revolver in his pocket.

John's state was less gracious. He was walking till he should tire himself out and his brain would cease to flinch at every face that looked so closely at him because he was going mad. If he walked for two hours and a half without halt, round and round the Parks, he might drug his mind by counting his paces till the rush of numbers would carry on awhile after he finished. At seven o'clock he re-entered the flat, and stared at his feet, while he raced through numbers from eleven thousand up. When he lifted his eyes, the black Thing he expected was pressed against the skirting board. The tonic the doctor had prescribed stood on a table. He drew the cork with his teeth, and gulped down to the first mark on the glass. He fancied he heard small, thumping sounds. Turning, it seemed to him that the Thing by the wall was working outwards.

Then there were two John Mardens – one dissolved by terror; the other, a long way off, detached, but as much in charge of him as he used to be of his underground shift at Messines.

'It's coming out into the room,' roared the first. 'Now you've *got* to go mad! Your pistol – before you make an exhibition of yourself!'

'Call it, you fool! Call it!' the other commanded.

'Come along! Good dog! Come along!' John whispered. Slowly, ears pressed to head, the inky blur crawled across the parquet on to the rug.

'Go-ood doggie! Come along, then!' John held out a clenched fist and felt, he thought, a touch of hellfire that would have sent him through the window, except for the second John, who said: – 'Right! All right! A cold nose is the sign of a well dog. It's all right! It's alive!'

'No. It's *come* alive!' shouted the first. 'It'll grow like the bullock in the cup! Pistol, you!'

'No – no – alive! Quite alive!' the other interrupted. 'It's licking your fist, and – nff! – it's made a mess in the corner – on the polished three-eighth-inch oak parquet, set on cement with brick archings. Shovel – *Not* pistol! Get the shovel, you ass!'

Then, John Marden repeated aloud: – 'Yes. It's made a mess. I'll get the shovel – shovel – steel – nickel-handled – one. Oh, you filthy little beast!'

He reached among the fire-irons and did what was necessary. The small thing, flat, almost, as a postage stamp, crawled after him. It was sorry, it whimpered. Indeed, it had been properly brought up, but circumstances had been too much for it, and it apologised – on its back. John stirred it with a toe. Feeling its amends had been accepted, it first licked and then rapturously bit his shoe.

'It's a dog right enough,' said John. He lifted a cracked voice and called aloud: – 'There *is* a dog here! I mean there's a dog here.'

As he remembered himself and leaned towards the bellpush, Shingle entered from the bedroom, where he had been laying out dinner kit, with a story of some badly washed shirts that seemed on his mind.

'But there's a dog –' said John.

Oh, yes! Now that John mentioned it, a pup had arrived at 5.15 p.m. – brought over from the dog shop by Mr Wilham himself who, having observed Captain Marden's interest in his windows, had taken the liberty of sending on approval – price fifteen guineas – one Dinah, jet-black Aberdeen of the dwarf type, aged five months and a fortnight, with pedigree attached to Mr Wilham's letter (on the mantelpiece, left when Mr Wilham found Captain Marden was not at home, sir) and which would confirm all the above statements. Shingle took his time to make everything clear, speaking in a tone that no man of his acquaintance had ever heard. He broke back often to the badly washed shirts, which, somehow, John found comforting. The pup ceased to grovel.

'Wilham was right about 'er breedin'. Not a white 'air on 'er! An' look at 'er boo-som frills!' said Shingle voluptuously.

Dinah, ears just prickable, sat on the floor between them, looking like a bandy-legged bat.

'But one can't keep dogs in these flats. It's forbidden, isn't it?' John asked.

'Me an' the janitor'll arrange that. Probert'll come in 'andy to take 'er walks, too.' Shingle mused aloud.

'But I don't know anything about dogs.'

'*She'll* look after all that. She's a bitch, you see, sir. An' so that'll be all right.'

Shingle went back to the evening kit.

John and Dinah faced each other before the fire. His feet, as he sat, were crossed at the ankles. Dinah moved forward to the crotch thus presented, jammed her boat-nosed head into it up to the gullet, pressed down her chin till she found the exact angle that suited her, tucked her forelegs beneath her, grunted, and went to sleep, warm and alive. When John moved, she rebuked him, and Shingle, ten minutes later, found him thus immobilised.

'H'sh!' said John.

But Dinah was awake and said so.

'Oh! That's it, is it?' Shingle grinned. 'She knows 'oo's what already.'

'How d'you mean?' John asked.

'She knows where I come in. She's yours. *I've* got to look after 'er. That's all. 'Tisn't as if she was a dog-pup.'

'Yes, but what am I to do about her?'

'We-ell, o' course, you must be careful you don't mix up with others. She's just the right age for distemper. She'll 'ave to be took out on the lead. An' then there'll be 'er basket an' sundries.'

John Marden did not attend, because in the corner, close to the skirting board, lay That Other, who had borne him company for the past few days.

'She – looks like a good ratter,' he stammered.

'I'd forgot that. 'Ere! Young lady!' said Shingle, following the line of John's eye. ''Ave you ever 'eard anything about rats?'

Dinah rose at once and signified that she had – lots.

'That's it, then! Rrrats! Rrats, ducky! Rrrout 'em out!'

She in turn followed the hint of Shingle's hand, scuttled to the corner indicated and said what she would have done had enemies been present. When she trotted back, That Other took shape again behind her, but John felt relieved.

'Now about dinner, sir!' said Shingle. 'It's 'er first night at 'ome. 'Twouldn't do to disappoint 'er, would it?'

'Bring something up here, then,' said John. 'I'll dress now.'

On Shingle's departure he rose and, followed by an interested Dinah, trod, not for the first time, firmly in the corners of his room. Then he went to dress. Dinah backed against the bath, the wisdom of centuries in her little solemn mask, till John's fluttering shirt-tails broke it all up. She leaped, grabbed them, and swung into John's calves. John kicked back. She retired under the bulge of the porcelain and told him what she thought of him. He sat down and laughed. She scolded till he dropped a stud, and the two hunted for it round the cork mat, and he was just able to retrieve it from between her teeth. Both sat down to meat, a little warm and dishevelled. That other watched them, but did not insist, though Dinah backed into him twice.

'I've made a temp'ry collar and lead off Probert. I'll take 'er for 'er last walk,' Shingle announced when he had cleared away.

'You will not,' said John. 'Give 'em to me.'

The upshot was some strenuous exercise in the Mall, when Dinah, to whom night and London were new, lassoed John twice and a stranger once, besides nearly choking when she was snatched from under the wheels of a car. This so saddened her that she sat down, and had to be brought home, languidly affectionate, in a taxi. As John said, the adventure showed she would not be afraid of cars.

'There's nothin' that young woman's afraid of, 'cept not bein' made much of,' Shingle replied. 'Green 'ud suit 'er better than red in collars. But I expect you'll do your own buyin', sir.'

'I will. You get the dog biscuit,' said John.

'Puppy biscuit!' said Shingle, deeply shocked, and he mentioned the only brand. 'A pup's like a child – all stummick.'

Going to bed was a riot. Dinah had no intention of being left out, and, when John moved a foot, tried to chew down to it through the blankets till she was admitted. Shingle, with the shaving water, would have given her her walk before breakfast next morning; but John took the duty, and she got muddy and had to be cleaned and dried on her return. Then, at Shingle's reminder, came the shopping expedition. John bought a green collar for Sunday, and a red for weekdays; two ditto leads; one wicker basket with green baize squab; two brushes, one toothed comb and one curry; and – Shingle sent him out again for these – pills, alterative, tonic, and antithelmintic. Ungrateful Dinah chewed the basket's varnished rim, ripped the bowels out of the squab, nipped Marden's inexperienced fingers as he gave her her first pill, and utterly refused to be brushed.

'Gawd!' said the agile Shingle, who was helping. 'Mother used to say a child was a noosance. Twins ain't in it with you, Dinah. An' now I suppose you'll 'ave to show 'em all off in your car.'

John's idea had been a walk down the Mall, but Shingle dwelt on the dangers of distemper and advised Richmond Park in, since rain was likely, the limousine. Dinah condescended a little when it came round, but hopped up into the right-hand seat, and gave leave to get under way. When they reached the Park she was so delighted that she clean forgot her name, and John chivvied her, shouting till she remembered. Shingle had put up a lunch, for fear, he explained, of hotels where ladies brought infectious Pekes, flown over for them by reprobate lovers in the Air Service; and after a couple of hours bounding through bracken, John appreciated the half-bottle of Burgundy that went with it. On their return, all Dinah's worldly pose dropped. 'I am,' she sniffed, 'but a small pup with a large nose. Let me rest it on your breast and don't you stop loving me for one minute.' So John slept too, and the chauffeur trundled them back at five o'clock.

'Pubs?' Probert demanded out of a corner of his mouth when John had gone indoors.

'Not in *ther* least,' said Shingle. 'Accordin' to our taxi man' – (Shingle did not love John's chauffeur) – 'Women and Song was 'is game. 'E says you ought to 'ave 'eard 'im 'owling after 'er. 'E'll be out in his own Hizzer-Swizzer in a week.'

'That's *your* business. But what about my commission on the price? You don't expect me to sanction dawgs 'ere for nothin'? Come *on!* It's all found money for you.'

John went drowsily up in the lift and finished his doze. When he waked, That Other was in his corner, but Shingle had found two tennis balls, with which Dinah was playing the Eton Wall Game by herself up and down the skirting board – pushing one with her nose, patting the other along with her paws, right through That Other's profiles.

'That shows she's been kitten-trained,' said Shingle. 'I'll bring up the janitor's and make sure.'

But the janitor's kitten had not been pup-trained and leaped on the table, to make sure. Dinah followed. It took all hands ten minutes to clear up the smashed glass of siphon, tumbler, and decanter, in case she cut her feet. The aftermath was reaped by a palpitating vacuum cleaner, which Dinah insisted was hostile.

When she and John and That Other in the corner sat it out after dinner, she discovered gifts of conversation. In the intervals of gossip she would seek and nose both balls about the room, then return to John's foot, lay her chin over it, and pick up where she had left off, in eloquent whimperings.

'Does she want anything?' he asked Shingle.

'Nothin', excep' not to be out of your mind for a minute. 'Ow about a bone now, Dinah?'

Out came her little pink tongue, sideways, there was a grunt and a sneeze, and she pirouetted gaily before the serving-man.

'Come downstairs, then,' he said.

'Bring it up here!' said John, sweeping aside Shingle's views on Bokhara rugs. This was messy – till Dinah understood that bones must be attended to on newspapers spread for that purpose.

These things were prelude to a month of revelations, in which Dinah showed herself all that she was, and more, since she developed senses and moods for John only. She was by turns, and in places, arrogant, imbecile, coy, forthcoming, jealous, exacting, abject, humorous, or, apparently, stone-cold, but in every manifestation adorable, and to be attended to before drinks. Shingle, as necessary to her comfort, stood on the fringe of her favours, but John was her Universe. And for her, after four weeks, he found himself doing what he had never done since Messines. He sang sentimental ditties – on his awful top notes Dinah would join in – such as:-

> 'Oh, show me a liddle where to find a rose
>   To give to ma honey chi-ile!
> Oh, show me a liddle where my love goes
>   An' I'll follow her all de while!'

At which she would caper, one ear up and one a quarter down. Then: –

> 'Ma love she gave me a kiss on de mouf,
>   An' how can I let her go-o?
> And I'll follow her norf, and I'll follow her souf,
>   Because I love her so!'

'Oo-ooo! Oooo!' Dinah would wail to the ceiling.

And then came calamity, after a walk in the Green Park, and Shingle said: – 'I told you so.' Dinah went off her feed, shivered, stared, ran at the nose, grew gummy round the eyes, and coughed.

'Ye-es,' said Shingle, rubbing his chin above her. 'The better the breed, the worse they cop it. Oh, damn the 'ole Air Force! It'll be a day-and-night job, I'm thinkin'. Look up a vet in the Directory? Gawd! *No!* This is distemper. I know a Canine Specialist and –'

He went to the telephone without asking leave.

The Canine Specialist was duly impressed by John and his wealth, and more effectively by Shingle. He laid down rules of nursing and diet which the two noted in duplicate, and split into watches round the clock.

'She 'as worked like a charm 'itherto,' Shingle confided to Probert, whose wife cooked for Dinah's poor appetite. 'She's jerked 'im out of 'isself proper. But if anythin' 'appens to 'er *now,* it'll be all Messines over again for 'im.'

'Did 'e cop it bad there, then?'

'Once, to my knowledge. I 'eard 'im before 'e went underground prayin' that 'is cup might parse. It 'ad come over 'im in an 'eap. Ye-es! It 'appens – it 'appens, as Mother used to say when we was young.'

'Then it's up to you to see nothing happens this time.'

''Looks it! But she's as jealous as a schoolteacher over 'im. Pore little bitch! Ain't it odd, though? She knows 'ow to play Weepin' Agnes with 'im as well as a woman! But she's cured 'im of lookin' in corners, an' 'e's been damnin' me something like 'olesome.'

John, indeed, was unendurably irritable while Dinah's trouble was increasing. He slept badly at first, then too heavily, between watches, and fussed so much that Shingle suggested Turkish baths to recover his tone. But Dinah grew steadily worse, till there was one double watch which Shingle reported to Probert as a 'fair curiosity'. 'I 'eard 'im Our Fatherin' in the bathroom when 'e come off watch and she 'adn't conked out.'

Presently there was improvement, followed by relapse, and grave talk of possible pneumonia. That passed too, but left a dreadful whimpering weakness, till one day she chose to patter back to life with her scimitar tail going like an egg-whisk. During her convalescence she had discovered that her sole concern was to love John Marden unlimitedly; to follow him pace by pace when he moved; to sit still and worship him when he stopped; to flee to his foot when he took a chair; to defend him loudly against enemies, such as cats and callers; to confide in, cherish, pet, cuddle, and deify without cease; and, failing that, to mount guard over his belongings. Shingle bore it very well.

'Yes, I know *you!*' he observed to her one morning when she was daring him to displace John's pyjamas from their bed. 'I'd be no good to you unless I was a puppy-biscuit. An' yet I *did* 'ave an' 'and in pullin' you through, you *pukka* little bitch, you.'

For some while she preferred cars to her own feet, and her wishes were gratified, especially in the Hizzer-Swizzer, which, with John at the wheel − you do not drink when you drive Hizzer-Swizzers − suited her. Her place was at his left elbow, nose touching his sleeve, until the needle reached fifty, when she had to throw it up and sing aloud. Thus, she saw much of summer England, but somehow did not recover her old form, in spite of Shingle's little doses of black coffee and sherry.

John felt the drag of the dull, warm days too; and went back to the Works for half a week, where he sincerely tried to find out what his secretary meant by plans for reorganisation. It sounded exactly like words, but conveyed nothing. Then he spent a night like that first one after Jerry Floyd had struck, and tried to deal with it by the same means; but found himself dizzily drunk almost before he began.

'The fuse was advarnced,' Shingle chuckled to Prohert. "E was like a boy with 'is first pipe. *An'* a virgin's 'ead in the mornin'! That shows the success of me treatment. But a man 'as to think of 'is own interests once-awhile. It's time for me Bank 'Oliday.'

'You an' your 'olidays. Ain't your bloke got any will of 'is own?'

'Not yet. 'E's still on the dole. 'Urry your Mrs P up with our medical comforts.'

That was Dinah's beef tea, and very good. But if you mix with it a few grains of a certain stuff, little dogs won't touch it.

'She's off 'er feed again,' said Shingle despairingly to John, whose coaxings were of no avail.

'Change is what you want,' said Shingle to her not quite under his breath. "Tain't fair to keep a dawg in town in summer. I ain't sayin' anythin' against the flat.'

'What's all that?' said John. Shingle's back was towards him.

'I said I wasn't sayin' anythin' against the flat, sir. A man can doss down anywhere – '

'Doss? I pay eight hundred a year for the thing!'

'But it's different with dawgs, sir, was all I was going to remark. Furniture's no treat to *them.*'

'She stays with me,' John snapped, while Dinah tried to explain how she had been defrauded of her soup.

'Of course she stays till she conks out.' Shingle removed the bowl funereally…

'No, I 'ave *not* pulled it off at one go,' he said to Probert. 'If you 'ad jest finished with seein' dawgs in corners, *you* wouldn't want to crash into society at a minute's notice, either. You'd think a bit before'and an' look round for a dry dugout. That's what we're doin'.'

Two days later, he dropped a word that he had a sister in the country, married to a cowkeeper, who took in approved lodgers. If anyone doubted the merits of the establishment, the Hizzer-Swizzer could get there in two hours, and make sure. It did so, and orders were given for the caravan to start next day, that not a moment might be lost in restoring Dinah.

She hopped out into a world of fields full of red-and-white bullocks, who made her (and John) flinch a little; and rabbits always on the edge of being run down. There was, too, a cat called Ginger, evidently used to dogs; and a dusty old collie, Jock, whom she snapped into line after five abject minutes.

'It suits 'er,' Shingle pronounced. 'The worst she'll catch off Jock is fleas. *Fairy Anne!* I've brought the Keatings.'

Dinah left Jock alone. Ginger, who knew all about rats and rabbits, was more to her mind, and those two ladies would work together along the brookside on fine, or through the barns on wet mornings, chaperoned by John and a nobby stick. She was bitten through the nose at her first attempt, but said nothing about it at the time, nor when she laid out the disinterred corpse in his bedroom – till she was introduced to iodine.

The afternoons were given to walks which began with a mighty huntress before her lord, standing on hind legs at every third bound to overlook the tall September grass, and ended with a trailing pup, who talked to John till he picked her up, laid her across his neck, a pair of small feet in each hand, and carried her drowsily licking his right cheek.

For evenings, there were great games. Dinah had invented a form of 'footer' with her tennis ball. John would roll it to her, and she returned it with her nose, as straight as a die, till she thought she had lulled him into confidence. Then angle and pace would change, and John had to scramble across the room to recover and shoot it back, if possible past her guard. Or she would hide (cheating like a child, the while) till he threw it into a corner, and she stormed after it, slipped, fetched up against the skirting board and swore. Last of all came the battle for the centre of the bed; the ferocious growling onsets; the kisses on the nose; the grunt of affectionate defeat and the soft jowl stretched out on his shoulder.

With all these preoccupations and demands, John's days slipped away like blanks beneath a stamping machine. But, somehow, he picked up a slight cold one Sunday, and Shingle, who had been given the evening off with a friend, had reduced the neglected whisky to a quarter bottle. John eked it out with hot water, sugar, and three aspirins, and told Dinah that she might play with Ginger while he kept himself housed.

He was comfortably perspiring at 7 p.m., when he dozed on the sofa, and only woke for Sunday cold supper at eight. Dinah did not enter with it, and Shingle's sister, who had small time-sense, said that she had seen her with Ginger mousing in the wash-house 'just now'. So he did not draw the house for her till past nine; nor finish his search of the barns, flashing his torch in all corners, till later. Then he hurried to the kitchen and told his tale.

'She've been wired,' said the cowman. 'She've been poaching along with Ginger, an' she've been caught in a rabbit-wire. Ginger wouldn't never be caught – twice. It's different with dogs *as* cats. That's it. Wired.'

'Where, think you?'

'All about the woods somewhere – same's Jock did when 'e were young. But 'e give tongue, so I dug 'im out.'

At the sound of his name, the old ruffian pushed his head knee-high into the talk.

'She'd answer *me* from anywhere,' said John.

'Then you'd best look for her. I'd go with 'ee, but it's foot-washin's for me tonight. An' take you a graf' along. I'll tell Shingle to sit up till you come back. 'E ain't 'ome yet.'

Shingle's sister passed him a rabbiting-spade out of the wash-house, and John went forth with three aspirins and some whisky inside him, and all the woods and fields under the stars to make choice of. He felt Jock's nose in his hand and appealed to him desperately.

'It's Dinah! Go seek, boy! It's Dinah! Seek!'

Jock seemed unconcerned, but he slouched towards the brook, and turned through wet grasses while John, calling and calling, followed him towards a line of hanging woods that clothed one side of the valley. Stumps presently tripped him, and John fell several times, but Jock waited. Last, for a long while, they quartered a full-grown wood, with the spotlight of his torch making the fallen stuff look like coils of half-buried wire between the lines. He heard a church clock strike eleven as he drew breath under the top of the rise, and wondered a little why a spire should still be standing. Then he remembered that this was England, and strained his ears to make sure that his calls were not answered. The collie nosed ground and moved on, evidently interested. John thought he heard a reply at last; plunged forward without using his torch, fell, and rolled down a steep bank, breathless and battered, into a darkness deeper than that of the woods. Jock followed him whimpering. He called. He heard Dinah's smothered whine – switched on the light and discovered a small cliff of sandstone ribbed with tree roots. He moved along the cliff towards the sound, till his light showed him a miniature canon in its face, which he entered. In a few yards the cleft became a tunnel, but – he was calling softly now – there was no doubt that Dinah lay somewhere at the end. He held on till the lowering roof forced him to knees and elbows and, presently, stomach. Dinah's whimper continued. He wriggled forward again, and his shoulders brushed either side of the downward-sloping way. Then every forgotten or hardly-held-back horror of his two years' underground work returned on him with the imagined weight of all earth overhead.

A handful of sand dropped from the roof and crumbled between his neck and coat collar. He had but to retire an inch or two and the pressure would be relieved, and he could widen the bottle-necked passage with his spade; but terror beyond all terrors froze him, even though Dinah was appealing somewhere a little ahead. Release came in a spasm and a wrench that drove him backward six feet like a prawn. Then he realised that it would be all to do again, and shook as with fever.

At last his jerking hand steadied on the handle of the spade.

He poked it ahead of him, at half arm's length, and gingerly pared the sides of the tunnel, raking the sand out with his hands, and passing it under his body in the old way of the old work, till he estimated, by torchlight, that he might move up a little without being pinned again. By some special mercy the tunnel beyond the section he had enlarged grew wider. He followed on, flashed once more, and saw Dinah, her head pressed close to the right-hand side of it, her white-rimmed eyes green and set.

He pushed himself forward over a last pit of terror, and touched her. There was no wire, but a tough, thumb-shaped root, sticking out of the sand-wall, had hooked itself into her collar, sprung backwards and upwards, and locked her helplessly by the neck. His fingers trembled so at first that he could not follow the kinks of it. He shut his eyes, and humoured it out by touch, as he had done with wires and cables deep down under the Ridge; grabbed Dinah, and pushed himself back to the free air outside.

There he was sick as never he had been in all his days or nights. When he was faintly restored, he saw Dinah sitting beside Jock, wondering why her Lover, King, and God did all these noisy things.

On his feet at last, he crawled out of the sandpit that had been a warren, badger's holt, and foxes' larder for generations, and wavered homeward, empty as a drum, cut, bruised, bleeding, streaked with dirt and raffle that had caked where the sweat had dried on him, knees bending both ways, and eyes unable to judge distance. Nothing in his working past had searched him to these depths. But Dinah was in his arms, and it was she who announced their return to the still-lighted farm at the hour of 1 a.m.

Shingle opened the door, and without a word steered him into the wash-house, where the copper was lit. He began to explain, but was pushed into a tub of very hot water, with a blanket that came to his chin, and a drink of something or other at his lips. Afterwards he was helped upstairs to a bed with hot bricks in it, and there all the world, and Dinah licking his nose, passed from him for the rest of the night and well into the next day again. But Shingle's sister was shocked when she saw his torn and filthy clothing thrown down in the wash-house.

''Looks as if 'e'd been spending a night between the lines, don't it?' her brother commented. "Asn't 'aif sweated either. Three hours of it, Marg'ret, an' rainin' on an' off. Must 'ave been all Messines with 'im till 'e found 'er.'

'An' 'e done it for 'is dog! What wouldn't 'e do for 'is woman!' said she.

'Yes. You *would* take it that way. I'm thinkin' about '*im*.'

'Ooh! Look at the blood. 'E must 'ave cut 'isself proper.'

'I went over 'im for scratches before breakfast. Even the iodine didn't wake 'im. 'Got 'is tray ready?'

Shingle bore it up, and Dinah's impenitent greeting of him roused her master.

'She wasn't wired. She knew too much for that,' were John's first words. 'She was hung up by her collar in an old bury. Jock showed me, an' I got her out. I fell about a bit, though. It was pitch-black; quite like old times.'

He went into details between mouthfuls, and Dinah between mouthfuls corroborated.

'So, you see, it wasn't her fault,' John concluded.

'That's what they all say,' Shingle broke in unguardedly.

'Do they? That shows they know Ginger. Dinah, you aren't to play with Ginger any more. Do you hear me?'

She knew it was reproof, as she flattened beneath the hand that caressed it away.

'Oh, and look here, Shingle.' John sat up and stretched himself. 'It's about time we went to work again. Perhaps you've noticed I have not been quite fit lately?'

'What with Dinah and all? – Ye-es, sir – a bit,' Shingle assented.

'Anyhow, I've got it off the books now. It's behind me.'

'Very glad to 'ear it. Shall I fill the bath?'

'No. We'll make our last night's boil do for today. Lay out some sort of town-kit while I shave. I expect my last night's rig is pretty well expended, isn't it?'

'There ain't one complete scarecrow in the 'ole entire aggregate.'

''Don't wonder. Look here, Shingle, I was underground a full half-hour before I could get at her. I should have said there wasn't enough money 'top of earth to make me do that over again. But I did. Damn it – I did! Didn't I, Dinah? *"Oh, show me a liddle where to find a rose."* Get off the bed and fetch my slippers, young woman! *"To give to ma honey chi-ile."* No; put 'em down; don't play with 'em!'

He began to strop his razor, always a mystery to Dinah. 'Shingle, this is the most damnable Government that was ever pupped. Look here! If I die tomorrow, they take about a third of the cash out of the Works for Death duties, counting four per cent interest on the money from the time I begin to set. That means one-third of our working capital, which is doing something, will be dug out from under us, so's these dam' politicians can buy more dole votes with it. An' I've got to waste my thinkin' time, which means making more employ-ment – (I say, this razor pulls like a road-scraper) – I've got to knock off my payin' work and spend Heaven knows how many days reorganising into companies, so that we shan't have our business knocked out if I go under. It's the *time* I grudge, Shingle. And we've got to make *that* up too, Dinah!'

The rasp of the blade on the chin set her tail thumping as usual. When he was dressed, she went out to patronise Jock and Ginger by the barn, where Shingle picked her up later, with orders to jump into the Hizzer-Swizzer at once and return to duty. She made her regulation walk round him, one foot crossing the other, and her tongue out sideways.

'Yes, *that's* all right, Dinah! You're a bitch! You're all the bitch that ever was, but you're a useful bitch. That's where you ain't like some of 'em. Now come and say goodbye to your friends.'

He took her to the kitchen to bid farewell to the cowman and his wife. The woman looked at her coldly as she coquetted with the man.

'She'll get 'er come-uppance one of these days,' she said when the car was reported.

'What for? She's as good a little thing as ever was. 'Twas Ginger's fault,' said the cowman.

'I ain't thinkin' of *her*,' she replied. 'I'm thinkin' she may 'ave started a fire that someone else'll warm at some fine day. It 'appens – it 'appens – as Mother used to say when we was all young.'

FOUR-FEET

I have done mostly what most men do,
And pushed it out of my mind;
But I can't forget, if I wanted to,
Four-Feet trotting behind,

Day after day, the whole day through –
Wherever my road inclined –
Four-Feet said, 'I am coming with you!'
And trotted along behind.

Now I must go by some other round –
Which I shall never find –
Somewhere that does not carry the sound
Of Four-Feet trotting behind.

'THY SERVANT A DOG'

Please may I come in? I am Boots. I am son of Kildonan Brogue – Champion Reserve VHC – very fine dog; and no-dash-parlour-tricks, Master says, except I can sit up, and put paws over nose. It is called 'Making Beseech'. Look! I do it out of own head. *Not* for telling... This is Flat-in-Town. I live here with Own God. I tell:

I

There is walk-in-Park-on-lead. There is off-lead-when-we come-to-the-grass. There is 'nother dog, like me, off lead. I say: 'Name?' He says: 'Slippers.' He says: 'Name?' I say: 'Boots.' He says: 'I am fine dog. I have Own God called Miss.' I say: 'I am very fine dog. I have Own God called Master.' There is walk-round-on-toes. There is Scrap. There is Proper Whacking. Master says: 'Sorry! Awfully sorry! All my fault.' Slipper's Miss says: 'Sorry! My fault too.' Master says: 'So glad it is both our faults. Nice little dog, Slippers.' Slipper's Miss says: 'Do you really think so?' Then I made 'Beseech'. Slipper's Miss says: 'Darling little dog, Boots.' There is on lead, again, and walking with Slippers behind both Own Gods, long times... Slippers is not-half-bad dog. Very like me. 'Make-fine-pair, Master says...

There is more walkings in Park. There is Slippers and his Miss in that place, too. Own Gods walk together – like on lead. We walk behind. We are tired. We yawn. Own Gods do not

look. Own Gods do not hear... They have put white bows on
our collars. We do not like. We have pulled off. They are bad to
eat...

II

Now we live at Place-in-Country, next to Park and plenty good
smells. We are all here. Please look! I count paws. There is me,
and Own God – Master. There is Slippers, and Slipper's Own
God – Missus. That is all my paws. There is Adar. There is
Cookey. There is James-with-Kennel-that-Moves. There is
Harry-with-Spade. That is all Slippers' paws. I cannot count
more; but there is Maids, and Odd-man, and Postey, and
Telegrams, and Pleasm-butcher and People. And there is
Kitchen Cat, which runs up Wall. *Bad! Bad! Bad!*

At morning-time Adar unties and brushes. There is going
quick upstairs past Cookey and asking Gods to come to
brekker. There is lie-down-under-the-table-at-each-end, and
heads-on-feets of Gods. Sometimes there is things-gived-
under table. But 'must *never* beg'.

After brekker, there is hunting Kitchen Cat all over garden
to Wall. She climbs. We sit under and sing. There is waiting for
Gods going walks. If it is nothing-on-their-tops, it is only
round the garden, and 'get-off-the-flower-beds-you-two!' If it
is wet, it is hearthrugs by fire, or 'who-said-you-could-sit on-
chairs-Little-Men?' It is always being with Own Gods – Own
Master and Own Missus. We are most fine dogs... There is
Tall far-off dog, which comes through laurels, and looks. We
have found him by own dustbin. We said: 'Come back, and
play!' But he wented off. His legs are all bendy. And wavy ears.
But bigger than Me!

III
AUGUST 1923

Please sit up! I will tell you by Times and Long Times – each
time at a time. I tell good things and dretful things.

Beginning of Times. There was walk with Own Gods, and 'basket-of-things-to-eat-when-we-sit-down – piggies.' It were long walks. We ate lots. After, there was rabbits which would not stay. We hunted. We heard sorrowful singing in woods. We went look-see. There was that far-off Tall dog, singing to hole in bank. He said: 'I have been here dretful long whiles, and I do not know where here is.' We said: 'Follow tails!' He followed back to Own Gods. Missus said: 'Oh, you poor big baby!' Master said: 'What on earth is Kent's puppy doing here?' Tall dog went on tum plenty, and said small. There was 'give-him-what's-left'. He kissed hands. We all wented home across fields. He said he were playing with washing-on-line, which waved like tails. He said little old dog with black teeth came, and said he would make him grow-into-a-hound, if he went with. So he wented with, and found beautiful Smell. Old dog said him to put his dash-nose-upon-the-ground and puzzle. He puzzled long ways with old dog. There was field full of 'ware-sheep and beautiful Smell stopped. Old dog was angry and said him to cast-forward. But Peoples came saying loud. He ran into woods. Old dog said if he waited long enough there he would grow-into-a-hound, and it would do-him-good to have to find his way home, because he would have to do it most of his life if he was so-dash-stoopid-as-all-that. Old dog went away and Tall dog waited for more beautiful Smell, and it was night-times, and he did not know where home was, and he singed what we heard. He were very sorry. He is quite new dog. He says he is called 'Dam-Puppy'. After long whiles there was smells which he knew. So he went through hedge and ran to his home. He said he was in-for-Proper-Whacking.

One Time after That. Kitchen Cat sits on Wall. We sing. She says: 'Own Gods are going away.' Slippers says: 'They come back at Biscuit-time.' Kitchen Cat says: 'This time they will go and *never* come back.' Slippers says: 'That is not real rat.' Kitchen Cat says: 'Go to top of House, and see what Adar is doing with kennels-that-shut.'

We go to top of House. There is Adar and kennels-that-shut. She fills with things off Gods' feets and tops and middles. We go downstairs. We do not understand...

Kitchen Cat sits on Wall and says: 'Now you have seen that Own Gods are going. Wait till kennels-that-shut are put behind kennel-that-moves, and Own Gods get in. Then you will know.' Slippers says: 'How do you know where that rat will run?' Kitchen Cat says: 'Because I am Cat. You are Dog. When you have done things, you ask Own Gods if it is Whack or Pat. You crawl on tum. You say: "Please, I will be good." What will you do when Own Gods go and never come back?' Slippers said: 'I will bite you when I catch you.' Kitchen Cat said: 'Grow legs!'

She ran down Wall and went to Kitchen. We came after. There was Cookey and broom. Kitchen Cat sat in window and said: 'Look at this Cookey. Sometimes this is thick Cookey; sometimes this is thin Cookey. But it is always my Cookey. I am never Cookey's Cat. But you must always have Own Gods with. Else you go bad. What will you do when Own Gods go away?' We were not comfy. We went inside House. We asked Own Gods not to go away and never come back. They did not understand...

IV

Time After. Own Gods *have* gone away in kennel-that-moves, with kennels-that-shut behind! Kennel came back at Biscuit-time, but no Gods. We went over House looking. Kitchen Cat said: 'Now you see!' We went to look everywhere. There was nothing... There is Peoples called Carpenters come. They are making a little House inside Big House. There is Postey talking to Adar. There is Pleasm-butcher talking to Cookey. There is everybody talking. Everybody says: 'Poor little chaps.' *And* goes away.

Some more Time. This night-time, Shiny Plate shined into our kennels, and made sing. We sang: 'When will Own Gods come back?' Adar looked out from high up above, and said: 'Stop that, or I'll come down to you.' We were quiet, but Shiny Plate shined more. We singed: 'We will be good when the Gods come back.' Adar came down. There was Whackings. We are poor little small dogs. We live in Outside Places. Nobody cares for.

V

Other more times. I have met that Tall far-off dog with large feet. He is not called 'Dam-Puppy'. He is called Ravager-son-of-Regan. He has no Own God because he will pass-the-bottle-round-and-grow-into-a-Hound. He lives across Park, at Walk, with dretful Peoples called Mister-Kent. I have wented to Walk. There were fine smells and pig-pups, and a bucket full of old things. Ravager said: 'Eat hearty!' He is nice dog. I ate lots. Ravager put his head through handle of bucket. It would not go away from him. He went back-first, singing. He sang: 'I am afraid.' Peoples came running. I went away. I wented into dark place called Dairy. There was butters and creams. People came. I went out of a little window. I sicked-up two times before I could run quick. I went to own kennel and lay down. That Peoples called Mister Kent came afterwards. He said to Adar: 'That little black beast is dam-thief.' Adar said: 'Nonsense! He is asleep.' Slippers came and said: 'Come and play Rats.' I said: 'Go to Walk and play with Ravager.' Slippers wented. People thought Slippers was me. Slippers came home quick. I am very fine dog but Master has not come back!

VI

After that Time. I am Bad Dog. I am Very Bad Dog. I am 'G'way-you-dirty-little-devil!' I found a Badness on the road. I liked it! I rolled in it! It were nice! I came home. There was Cookey and Adar. There was 'Don't-you-come-anigh-me.' There was James-with-kennel-that-moves. There was: 'Come 'ere, you young polecat!' He picked up, and washed with soap, and sticky water out of kennel-that-moves rubbed into all my hairs. There was tie-up. I smelled very bad to myself. Kitchen Cat came. I said: 'G'way! I am Filfy Bad Dog! I am Proper Stinkpot!' Kitchen Cat said: 'That is not your own rat. You are bad because Own Gods do not come back. You are like Peoples who cannot be good without Own Gods to pat.'

VII

Other Fresh Times. Now I am great friend of Ravager. Slippers and me have wented to hunt Hen at Walk. She were angry Hen-lady with pups. She bit Slippers, two times, with her nose, under his eye. We all went one way. There was Pig-lady with pups that way. We went other way. There was Mister-Kent-Peoples with whack-stick that way. We wented more ways, quick. We found a fish head on a heap of nice old things. There was Ravager. We all went for play. There was cow-pups in field. They ran after. We went under gate and said. They ran away. We ran after till they stopped. They turned round. We went away again. They ran after. We played a long while. It were fun. Mister-Kent-People and more Peoples came calling dretful names. We said to Ravager: 'We will go home.' Ravager said: 'Me too.' He ran across field. We went home by small ditches. We played Rat-sticks on the lawn.

Cowman Peoples came and said to Adar: 'Those two little devils have been chasing pounds off the calves!' Adar said: 'Be ashamed of yourself! Look at 'em! Good as gold!' We waited till Peoples were gone. We asked for sugar. Adar gave. Ravager came through laurels – all little. He said: 'I have had Proper Whacking. What did you get?' We said: 'Sugar.' He said: 'You are very fine dogs. I am hungry.' I said: 'I will give you my store-bone in the border. Eat hearty.' He digged. We helped. Harry-with-Spade came. Ravager went through laurels like Kitchen Cat. We got Proper Whacking and tie-up for digging in borders... When we are bad, there is Sugar. When we are good, there is Whack-whack. That is same rat going two wrong ways...

VIII

Harry-with-Spade has brought a Rat… Look, please! Please look! I am Rrreal Dog! I have killed a Rat. I have slew a Rat! He bit me on the nose. I bit him again. I bit him till he died. I shookened him dead! Harry said: 'Go-ood boy! Born ratter!' I am very-fine-dog-indeed! Kitchen Cat sat on the Wall and said: 'That is not your own Rat. You killed it to please a God.' When my legs are grown, I will kill Kitchen Cat like Rats. *Bad! Bad! Bad!*

IX

Time soon After. I wented to Walk to tell my friend Ravager about my Rat, and find more things to kill. Ravager said: 'There is 'ware-sheep for me, and there is 'ware-chicken for me, but there is no 'ware-Bull for me. Come into Park and play with Bull-in-yard.' We went under Bull's gate in his yard. Ravager said: 'He is too fat to run. Say!' I said. Bull said. Ravager said. Slippers said. I got under water trough and said dretful things. Bull blew with nose. I went out through fence, and came back through another hole. Ravager said from other side of yard. Bull spun. He blew. He was too fat. It were fun. We heard Mister-Kent saying loud. We went home across Park. Ravager says I am True Sporting Dog, only except because of my little legs.

X
OCTOBER 1923

Bad Times dead. Sit up! Sit up now! I tell! I tell! There has been washings and Sunday collars. Carpenter Peoples has gone away, and left new Small House inside Big House. There is very small kennel-that-rocks inside Small House. Adar showed. We went to James's house. He were gone away with kennel-that-moves. We went to front gate. We heard! We saw! Own Gods – very Own Gods – Master – Missus – came back!

We said. We danced. We rolled. We ran round. We went to tea, heads-on-feets of Own Gods! There were buttered toasts gived under table, and two sugars each...

We heard New Peoples talking in Big House. One Peoples said: 'Angh! Angh!' very small like cat-pups. Other Peoples said: 'Bye-loe! Bye-loe!' We asked Own Gods to show. We went upstairs to Small House. Adar was giving cup-o'-tea to New Peoples, more thick than Adar, which was small-talk inside kennel-that-rocks. It said: 'Aie! Aie!' We looked in. Adar held collars. It were *very* Small Peoples. It opened its own mouth. But there was no teeth. It waved paw. I kissed. Slippers kissed. New Thick, which is that Nurse, said: 'Well-Mum-I-never!' Both Own Gods sat down by Smallest Peoples and said and said and kissed paw. Smallest Peoples said very loud. New Thick gave biscuit in a bottle. We tail-thumped on floor, but 'not-for-you-greedies'. We went down to hunt Kitchen Cat. She ran up apple tree. We said: 'Own Gods *have* come back, with one Smallest New Peoples, in smallest-kennel!' Kitchen Cat said: 'That is not Peoples. That is Own Gods' Very Own Smallest. *Now* you are only dirty little dogs. If you say too loud to me or Cookey, you will wake that Smallest, and there will be Proper Whackings. If you scratch, New Thick will say: "Fleas! Fleas!" and there will be more Proper Whackings. If you come in wet, you will give Smallest sneezes. *So* you will be pushed Outside, and you will scratch at doors that shut-in-your-eye. You will belong with Yards and Brooms and Cold Passages and all the Empty Places.' Slippers said: 'Let us go to Own Kennel and lie down.' We wented.

We heard Own Gods walking in garden. They said: ''Nice to be home again, but where are the Little Men?' Slippers said: 'Lie still, or they will push us into the Empty Places.' We lay still. Missus called: 'Where is Slippers?' Master called: 'Boots, you ruffian! Hi! Boots!' We lay still. Own Gods came into yard and found. They said: 'Oh, *there* you are! Did you think we would forget you? Come-for-walks.' We came. We said soft. We rolled before feets, asking not to be pushed into Empty Places. I made a Beseech, because I were not comfy. Missus said: 'Who'd have thought they'd take it this way, poor Little Men?' Master threw plenty sticks. I picked up and brought back. Slippers went inside with Missus. He came out quick. He said: 'Hurry! Smallest is being washed.' I went like rabbits. Smallest was all no-things on top or feets or middle. Nurse, which is Thick, washed and rubbed, and put things on-all-over afterwards. I kissed hind feet. Slippers too. Both Gods said: 'Look – it tickles him! He laughs. *He* knows they're all right!' Then they said and they said and they kissed and they kissed it, and it was bye-lo – same as 'kennel-up' – and then dinner, and heads-on-feets under table, and lots things-passed-down. One were kidney, and two was cheeses. We are most fine dogs!

XI
MARCH 1924

Very many Long Times after those Times. Both Gods have gone-week-ends in kennel-that-moves. But we are not afraid. They will come back. Slippers went up to talk to that Smallest and Nurse. I went to see my great friend Ravager at Walk, because I see him very often. There was new, old, small, white dog outside Barn. There was only one eye. He was dretful bitted all over. His teeth was black. He walked slow. He said: 'I am Pensioned Hunt Terrier! Behave, you lapdog!' I was afraid of his oldness and his crossness. I went paws-up. I told about me and Slippers and Ravager. He said: 'I know that puppy. I taught him to grow-into-a-hound. I am more dash-old than Royal, his grandfather.' I said: 'Is it good Rat? He is my friend. Will he grow-into-a-Hound?' Hunt Terrier said: 'That depends.' He scratched his dretful-bitted neck and looked me out of his eye. I did not feel comfy. I wented into Barn. There was Ravager on Barn floor and two Peoples. One was all white, except his black ends, which was called Moore. One was long, proper man, and nice, which was called m'Lord. Moore-man lifted Ravager's head and opened his mouth. Proper Man looked. Moore said: 'Look, m'lord. He's swine-chopped.' Proper Man said: ''Pity! He's by Romeo and Regan.' Moore-man said: 'Yes, and she's the wisest, worst-tempered bitch ever was.' Proper Man gave Ravager biscuit. Ravager stood up stiff on toes – *very* fine dog. Moore said: 'Romeo's shoulders. Regan's feet. It's a pity, m'lord.' Proper Man said: *'And* Royal's depth. 'Great pity. *I* see. I'll give you the order about him tomorrow.'

They wented away. Ravager said: 'Now they will make me grow-into-a-Hound. I will be sent into Kennels, and schooled for cubbing-in-September.' He went after Hunt Terrier came and showed black teeth. I said: 'What is "swine-chopped"?' He said: 'Being snipey-about-the-nose, stoopid.' Then Moore came and put Hunt Terrier up on neck, same as Cookey carries Kitchen Cat. Hunt Terrier said: 'Never walk when you can ride at *my* time of life.' They wented away. Me too. *But* I were not comfy.

When I got home, Nurse and Adar and Cookey were in scullery, all saying loud about Slippers and Kitchen Cat and Smallest. Slippers were sitting in sink – bleedy. Adar turned sink-tap-water on his head. Slippers jumped down and ran. We hid in boot-house. Slippers said: 'I wented up to see that Smallest. He was bye-lo. I lay under Nurse's bed. She went down for cup-o'-tea. Kitchen Cat came and jumped into kennel-that-rocks, beside Smallest. I said: "G' out of this!" She said: "I will sleep here. It is warm." I said very loud. Kitchen Cat jumped out on floor. I bit her going to the door. She hit. I shook. We fell downstairs into Nurse. Kitchen Cat hit across face. I let go because I did not see. Kitchen Cat said, and Cookey picked up. I said, and Adar picked up, and put me on sink and poured water on bleedy eye. Then they all said. But I am quite well-dog, and it is *not* washing day for me.' I said: 'Slippers, you *are* fine dog! I am afraid of Kitchen Cat.'

111

Slippers said: 'Me too. But that time I was new dog inside-me. I were 'normous f'rocious big Hound! Now I am Slippers.'

I told about Ravager and Moore and Proper Man and Hunt Terrier and swine-chopped. Slippers said: 'I cannot see where that Rat will run. I smell it is bad rat. But I must watch my Smallest. It is your Rat to kill.'

XII

Next Time after Not-Comfy. Kitchen Cat is gone away and not come back. Kitchen is not nice to go in. I have went to see my friend Ravager at Walk. He were tied up. He sang sorrowful. He told dretful things. He said: 'When I were asleep last night, I grew-into-a-Hound – very fine Hound. I went sleep-hunting with 'nother Hound – lemon-and-white Hound. We sleep-hunted 'normous big Fox-Things all through Dark Covers. Then I fell in a pond. There was a heavy thing tied to my neck. I went down and down into pond till it was all dark. I were frightened and I unsleeped. Now I am not comfy.' I said: 'Why are you tied up?' He said: 'Mister-Kent has tied me up to wait for Moore.' I said: 'That is not my Rat. I will ask Hunt Terrier.'

So I went back into Park. I were uncomfy in all my hairs because of my true friend Ravager. There were hedgehog in ditch. He rounded up. I said loud. Hunt Terrier came out of bushes and pushed him into a wetness. He unrounded. Hunt Terrier killed. I said: 'You are most wonderful, wise, strong, fine dog.' He said: 'What bone do you want now, Snipey?' I said: 'Tell me, what is "snipey-about-the-nose"?' He said: 'It is what they kill Hound puppies for, because they cannot eat fast or bite hard. It is being like *your* nose.' I said: 'I can eat and bite hard. I am son of Champion Kildonan Brogue – Reserve – VHC – very-fine-dog.' Hunt Terrier said: 'I know that pack. They hunt fleas. What flea is biting you?' I said: 'Ravager is uncomfy, and I am uncomfy of my friend Ravager.' He said: 'You are not so lapdog as you look. Show me that puppy on the flags.' So I said about Ravager sleep-hunting and falling in pond, which he had told me when he were tied up. Hunt Terrier said: 'Did he sleep-hunt with a lemon-and-white-bitch with a scar on her left jowl?' I said: 'He said he hunted with 'nother Hound – lemon-and-white – but he did not say Lady-Hound or jowels. How did you know?' Hunt Terrier said: '*I* knew last night. It will be dash-near-squeak for Ravager.'

Then we saw Moore on Tall Horse in Park. Hunt Terrier said: 'He is going to the Master for orders about Ravager. Run!' I were runnier than Hunt Terrier. He was rude. There was Big House in Park. There was garden and door at side. Moore went in. Hunt Terrier stayed to mind Horse, which was his Tall Friend. I saw Proper Man inside, which had been kind to Ravager at Walk. So I wented in, too. Proper Man said: 'What's this, Moore? 'Nother Hunt Terrier?' Moore said: 'No, m'lord. It's that little black devil from The Place, that's always coming over to Kent's and misleading Ravager.' Proper Man said: 'No getting away from Ravager this morning, it seems.' Moore said: 'No—nor last night either, m'lord.' Proper Man said: 'Yes, I heard her.' Moore said: 'I've come for orders about Ravager, m'lord. 'Proper Man sat look-not-see – same as Master with pipe. I were not comfy. So I sat up on my end, and put paws over nose, and made a big Beseech. That is all I can. Proper Man looked and said: 'What? Are *you* in it too, you little oddity?' Hunt Terrier said outside: 'No dash-parlour tricks in there! Come on out of it!' So I came out and helped mind Tall Horse.

After whiles, Moore came out, and picked up Hunt Terrier, and put him on front saddle, and hurried. Hunt Terrier said rudenesses about my short legs. When we got to Walk, Moore said loud to Mister-Kent: 'It is all right.' Mister-Kent said: 'Glad of it. How did it come about?' Moore said: 'Regan saved him. She was howling cruel last night; and when his Lordship looked in this morning, she was all over him, playing the kitten and featherin' and pleadin'. *She* knew! He didn't say anything then, but he said to me just now: 'Ravager will be sent to Kennels with the young entry, and we'll hope his defect ain't-too-heredity.'

Mister-Kent untied. Ravager rolled and said and said and played with me. We played I were Fox-at-his-home-among-the-rocks, all round Pig-ladies-houses. I went to ground under hen house. Hen-ladies said plenty. Hunt Terrier said if he had me for two seasons, he would make me earn-my-keep. But I would not like. I am afraid I would be put-in-ponds and sunk, because I am snipey-about-the-nose. But now I am comfy in all my hairs. I have ate grass and sicked up. I am happy dog.

XIII
EARLY APRIL 1924

Most wonderful Times. We are fine dogs. There was Bell-Day, when Master comes black-all-over, and walks slow with shiny box on top and 'don't-you-play-with-my-brolly'. That is *always* Bell-Day Rat. Nurse put Smallest into push-kennel, and went for walk-in-Park. We went with, and ran, and said lots. We went by Walk all along railings of Park. Ravager heard. He said: 'I will come. My collar is too big.' He slipped collar and came with. That Smallest said loud and nice, and waved paw. Ravager looked into push-kennel and kissed Smallest on its face. Nurse shooed and wiped with hanky. Ravager said: '*Why* am I "slobbery-beast"? It is not 'ware-Smallest for me.'

We all walked across Park beside push-kennel. There was noise behind bushes. Bull-which-we-played-with-in-yard came out, and digged with paws and waved tail. Nurse said: 'Oh, what shall I do – I do? My legs are wobbly.' She took Smallest out of push-kennel and ran to railings. Bull walked quick after. We ran in front. Slippers and I said lots. Ravager jumped at his nose and ran. Bull spun. Ravager ran behind push-kennel. Bull hit push-kennel on one side, and kneeled-down-on. Ravager jumped at his nose, and Slippers bit behind. Me too. Bull spun.

Ravager ran a little in front. Bull came after to shrubbery. Ravager said: 'Chop him in cover!' We chopped, running in and out. Then Ravager bited and jumped back-with-barks before nose. It was fun. Bull got bleedy. Slippers and me said dretful things. Bull ran away into Park and stopped. We said from three places, so he could not choose which. It were great fun.

Peoples called out from railings round Walk. There was Nursey paws-up on ground, kicking feet. There was that Smallest and Own Gods holding tight. There was Mister-Kent-Peoples. Bull said, quite small – like cow-pup. Mister-Kent came and put stick at Bull's nose and took away on-lead. All the Peoples on the railing said most loud at us. We were frightened, because of chasing-pounds-off-those-calves. We went home other ways. Ravager came with, because he had slipped his collar and was in for Proper-Whack-Whack. I opened dustbin with my nose – like I can do. There were porridge and herring-tails and outsides of cheeses. It was nice. Then Ravager stuck up his back hairs most dretful, and said: 'If I am for Proper Whackings, I will chop Mister-Kent.' We went with to see.

There was plenty Peoples there, all Bell-Day-black all over. We saw Moore. We saw Mister-Kent. He was bleedy one side his blacks. He blew. He said 'Ravager's made a proper hash of him. Look at me Sunday best!' Moore said: 'That shows he ain't swine-chopped to matter.' Mister-Kent said: 'Dam'-all-how-it-shows! What about my Bull?' Moore said: 'Put him down to the Poultry Fund; for if ever Bull cried dunghill, *he* did with Ravager.' Mister-Kent said plenty-lots.

Ravager walked slow round barn and stopped stiff. His back hairs was like angry Gentlemen-pigs. Mister-Kent began to say dretful. Moore said: 'Keep away. He has his mother's temper, and it's dash-awkward.' Then Moore said nice small things and patted. Ravager put his head on Moore's feets, and all his back hairs lay down and was proper coat again. Moore took him to kennel, and filled water trough, and turned straw on sleeping bench. Ravager curled up like small puppy, and kissed hands. Moore said: 'Let him be till he sees fit to come out. Else there'll be more hurt than your Bull.'

Slippers and me ran away. We was afraid. We were dretful dirty. My nice frilly drawers was full of sticky burrs, and our front-shirts were bleedy off Bull. So we went to our Adar, but Own Gods and Smallest and Nurse Thick came, and they all said and said and petted, except Cookey because Kitchen Cat is not come back. There was wonderful things-under-table at dinner. One was liver. One was cheese-straw and one was sardine. Afterwards, was coffee-sugar. We wented up to see Smallest bye-loed. He is quite well. We are *most* fine dogs. Own Gods keep saying so. It are fun!

Just after that Times. There is no more Ravager at Walk. I have wented to see him. Moore came with Tall Horse and cracky-whip and took. Ravager showed very proud dog inside (he said), but outside frightened puppy. He said I were his true friend in spite of my little legs. He said he will come again when he is grown-into-a-Hound, and I will always be his True Small Friend. He went looking back, but Moore cracked whip. Ravager sung dretful. I heard him all down the lane after I could see. I am sorrowful dog, but I am always friend of my friend Ravager. Slippers came to meet me at Rabbit Holes. We got muddy on tum, because we have low clearances. So we went to our Adar for clean.

Kitchen Cat was on Wall again. Slippers said: 'Give her cold-dead-rat.' We wented-past-under quite still. She said: 'I am Kitchen Cat come back, silly little pups!' We did not say or look. We went to Adar. Slippers said me: 'Now we hunt Bulls in Parks, do not ever say to Kitchen Cat – *ever!*' I said: 'Good rat! You *are* wise dog.' Cookey picked up and said: 'Mee own precious Pussums!' Kitchen Cat said: 'I am Cat, not Dog, drat you!' Cookey kept on petting. Then she tied up by basket in kitchen, and said: 'Now you've had your lesson about going up

to the nursery, you'll stay with me in future and behave!'
Kitchen Cat spitted. Cookey took broom in case we hunted; but
we went past quite still. This is finish to Kitchen Cat. We are
fine dogs. We hunt Bulls. She does not hunt real rats. She is
Bad! Bad! Bad!

XIV
LATE APRIL 1925

Most Wonderful Times. This is me – Boots. Three years old. I
am 'sponsible dog (Slippers, too), Master says. We are
'sponsible for that Smallest. He can get out of push-kennel. He
walks puppy-way between Slippers and me. He holds by ears
and noses. When he sits down, he pulls up same way. He says:
'Boo-boo!' That is me. He says: 'See-see!' That is Slippers. He
has bitted both our tails to make his teeth grow strong, because
he has no bone at night. *We* did not say. He has come into both
our kennels, and tried to eat our biscuit. Nurse found. There
was smallest Whack-Whacks. *He* did not say. He is finest
Smallest that is.

He had washings and new collar and extra brush. It was *not*
Bell-Day. It was after last-run-of-season. He walked on lawn.
We came, one each side. He held. There was horns in Park. I
were tingly in all my hairs. But I did not say. (Too old to make-
fool-of-myself, *my* time of life, Master says.) There was
Hounds and Pinks coming on grass. There was Moore – but he
was Pinks. There was Mister-Kent. But he was like rat-catcher,
Hunt Terrier said. There was nice Proper Man which was kind
to Ravager in barn about being swine-chopped. There was
some more Pinks, but not friends. Moore took all Hounds to
gate by lawn. They sat down quiet. They was beautiful muddy,
and seeds in coats and tails, and ears bleedy. Hunt Terrier sat
in own basket on Tall Horse. When Moore put him down he
said dretful things to Hounds. They did not say back. Proper
Man said to Master and Missus: 'We have come to call with
brush for that Smallest.'

Smallest liked because it tickled; but Nurse Thick washed off with hanky quick. Master-an'-Missus said: 'How did Ravager do?' Proper Man said: 'As usual. Led from end to end. He wants to talk to you.' Ravager stood up tall at the gate and put nose through. Smallest stretched out and Ravager kissed. Then Moore said: 'Over, lad!' Ravager overed in one jump, and said to Smallest, two times most loud, like Bell-Day, and played puppy very careful, and let Smallest hold by ears. His ears was all made round.

He spoke me. I went paws-up, because he were so big and dretful and strong. He said: 'Drop it, Stoopid! 'Member me bein' lost? 'Member Bucket and Fishheads? 'Member Bull? 'Member Cow-pups and Lady-pigs and Mister-Kent and Proper Whackings and all those things at Walk? You are True Sporting Dog, except only because of your little legs, and always true friend of Ravager.' He rolled me over, and held down with paws, and play-bit in my neck. I play-bitted him too, right on jowels! *All* the Hounds saw! I walked round stiff-on-toes, *most* proud.

Then Hunt Terrier wiggled under gate without leave. Proper Man said to Missus: 'He is pensioned now, but it would break his heart not to turn out with the rest. He can't hurt your dogs, poor fellow.' Hunt Terrier walked-on-toes round me and showed black teeth. I went paws-up, because he were old and dretful about knowing Uncomfy things. He said: 'I will let you off this time, Snipey, because you knew about Ravager sleep-hunting in Dark Covers. 'Dash narrow shave, that! Now I must go and look after the young entry. Not one-dash-Hound among 'em!'

He went away and bitted at an old Lady-Hound, lemon-and-white, with black bites on jowels. She said, and wrinkled nose dretful, but she did not chop. She sat and looked at Ravager through gate, and said to him – like Bell-Day, but more loud. Proper Man said: 'Old Regan wants her tea. 'Fraid we must be going.' They wented away. There was horns and

Horses and Pinks, and Hounds jumping up, and Moore saying names loud, and Ravager overed gate most beautiful. They wented all away – all – all. I were very small little dog.

Then Smallest said: 'Boo-boo!' 'See-see!' He took necks by collars. He said to Own Gods: 'Look! Look! Own 'ounds! Own 'ounds! Tum on tea, 'ounds.'...

Please, that is finish for now of all about me-and-Slippers. I make Beseech!

THE GREAT PLAY HUNT

Please! Door! Open Door!... This is me – Boots – which told you all those things about my true friend Ravager at Walk and Mister-Kent-Peoples and Kitchen Cat and Master-Missus and Smallest, when I were almost Pup. Now I am 'sponsible dog, rising eight. I know all about Peoples' talkings. No good saying r-a-t-s or w-a-l-k-s to me. I know! (Slippers too.)

Slippers is 'sponsible for Smallest, risen seven and a half, because Smallest belongs to Missus. And Slippers too. I help. It is very fine Smallest. It has sat on Tall Horse, which is called Magistrate, in front of that White Man which was kind to Ravager at Walk, which I told you, which is called Moore-Kennel-Huntsman. It has learned to keep hands down and bump, and fall off proper, and all those things. Now he has own pony called Taffy-was-a-Welshman. He rides with Moore and Magistrate all-over-Park. We come with. *And* he goes to Meet when it is at Kennels. Master-Missus say he must not real-hunt-just-yet. He does not like and says. I come to Meets with James in kennel-that-moves because of those dash new Hunt Terriers. I speak to my friend Ravager from next to steering wheel, where I sit. He is best-hound-ever-was, Moore says. He walks close to near foreleg of Magistrate. It is *most* 'sponsible place. He has nigh-half-choked Upstart for trying to take it, Moore says.

Now I will tell things and things like rats running.

120

First, 'was dash-bad business about Smallest in Old Nursery before brekker. There was hard tight collar. That new Nursey, which is called Guvvy, pinched under neck. Smallest said about boney old Lady-Hound. Guvvy said-and-said and shook Smallest. We shook too – one each side her middle dress. We did *not* nip. It tore of herself. Missus came up quick. Guvvy said all-about-all again. We wented downstairs quick. Missus called to Master. He said: 'Come here, you two sweeps!' There was Proper Whacking with own cutty-whip. But we did *not* nip that Guvvy. There was whack-whack for Smallest too. He was put in corner till 'I-am-sorry.' We went with to sit by, same as always with old Nursey. Missus said: 'I will not have my son's education perverted by two 'sreputable curs.' There was order not to be with Smallest all whole day. *And* nothing gived under-table at brekker. So we wented to dustbin, which I can open with my nose. House not comfy because of Guvvy saying about us to our Adar. Our Adar said: 'P'raps I ought to have warned you, but now you have had your lesson. Of course, Slippers will never forgive you for touching Master Digby, and as for that Boots, he can bear malice for months!' After dustbin I said Slippers: 'Come for walkabout.' He said: 'Own-God-Master always wants you help him walkabout after brekker.' I said: 'I do not want Own God. I did *not* nip that Guvvy-Lady-Hound. Come with.' Slippers said: 'They have put soap on my Smallest's teeth for bad-wording. He is kennelled up in Old Nursery. I will stay at home. P'raps he will wave me out of window.' So I took myselfs to Walk, where Mister-Kent-Peoples is. I were nice to Mister-Kent's two Frilly Smalls, which I know since they came. There was bread and butter and sugar. There was: 'Run along to school now, dearies.' I wented with to take care. There was lots more Smalls going to school, which I all knew. I ran sticks for them. There was two pieces gingerbread and two sweeties. Then I wented back to Walk because I were hungry. There was two hen-heads outside ferret-kennel box. They were nice. There was Lady-Hen in barn hatching eggs. They were good. There was Ben-sheep-dog, which was tied up because of meddy that morning. He had left his bone out too far. I took away to Micefield where Wood's Edge comes down behind Walk. I caught four mices by jumping-on through grass. There was some of very old rabbit lying about. But bad fur. So I unhad all which was inside me, and wented into Woods for drink in Middle Ride. *And* sleeped. When I unsleeped, there was that old Fox which Ravager calls Tags, because he has very fine brush. He is dash-old but dash-wise, Ravager says. There was steel trap on near fore. He was biting-out foot. He said: 'If I am found like this, it is finish-for-me.' I said: 'There is no Meet today.' He said: 'Every day is Meet for that dash-Ben-cur-dog.' I said: 'Ben is tied up. He has took meddy.' Tags said: 'Then there is a chance.' He bited his foot, same as me with thorns. He bited off two toes, and licked and licked. He said: 'Serves me right for being dash-fool, my time-of-life.' He said it were two-nice-kind-ladies, long ways off, across railway line in Cotswold country (because Tags does *not* kill at home), which took hens to be killed in kennels-that-move, which had set trap under hen-house floor, with chicken which he could see. He tried to rake out. Trap caught two toes. He came home with – four miles – all through the night-times. He said he could not kill for himself for long whiles now, because of sore toes. I said: 'There is a big bone and four mices in Micefield, and some of old rabbit.' He said: 'Good enough! Tell Ravager I am as lame as trees. I am two toes short. I will lie up for rest of season. Then I will go to my-home-among-the-rocks-in-Wales, if I can keep living alive.'

I wented back to Walk, because I were hungry again. Ben said me lots about his bone. I said back. I danced. A Kent Frilly Small came and said: 'There is Boots playing so pretty with Ben. May I take him home, in case he will lose himself?' I were very nice. But first was tea in Kent-kitchen with Frilly Smalls – bread and ham-juice. Then I took that Frilly back careful to own back door. Adar said: 'Lost? Him? Boots? *Never,* me dear!' Own Gods was at tea. But not Smallest. Slippers sat close by door making sorrowful sniffles which Own Gods do not like. (I helped.) Master said: 'Dash-it-all, if the house is to be run by this blackguard Trades Union of ours, accept it. Have Digby down!' Smallest came down to tea. We was all-over-him. There was teacake and two sugars and ginger-biscuits. Missus said: 'Do you think Boots spent the whole day looking for Smallest?' Master said: 'Not if I know Boots.' Own Gods began talking Master-Missus way. We wented to help Smallest kennel-up. I played smelling rats and looking rat-holes in Old Nursery. I ran about and growled dretful. Guvvy did not like because of her feet. But I did *not* ever nip that Guvvy – more than Tags ever killed at Walk. (Slippers too.) 'Was dash silly business for me afterwards – my time-o'-life. Guvvy told Missus about rat-holes. Missus told Master. Master told James to look and stop rat-holes. James told Old Nursery was tight as bottles everywhere. Adar said me in scullery after: 'Boots, you come along o' me.' I wented up with. I were not comfy. Adar said: 'Now you find those precious rat-holes of yours.' I played looky-sniffy hard. But it were play rat-holes. I went paws-up. Adar said: 'I thought so, you little devil!' She took by collar and rubbed nose hard in corner, same as if I were pup being taught House. I were very angry. I wented under bed. She pulled me out by tail. She said: 'You black-hearted little villain! But I love yer for it!' *And* she kissed me same as Small Pup. I were dretful 'shamed. But I did not *ever* nip that Guvvy.

Now I tell new things. *Please* sit up!

There was plenty-rides always with Smallest and Moore in Park. Smallest wanted to real-hunt dretful bad, but Master-Missus said not-just-yet-awhile. Moore did not say except to James at Meet, when Smallest tried to quick-up that Taffy with safety pin. Moore saw. He said James: 'My money is on the young entry.' I said Ravager all those things, which Tags had told me about his sore toes. Ravager said: 'Tell Tags I am dash-sorry for him. He has given me as much as I could do for five seasons, and he was not chickens then. I hope he will lie-at-earth till leaves-on, because business is business.' Next whiles I was at Middle Ride I told Tags what Ravager had said. Tags said his toes was not so sore, and if it were early spring, he could keep living alive – somehow.

Time whiles after that, 'was Meet at Kennels. Master-Missus said Smallest could begin real hunting at cubbing-times next September. Smallest was dretful good, and talked Master-Missus and Slippers how he would hunt, till bedtime. I told my friend Ravager all those things, when I speaked loud to him next Meet, before all the Hounds. He said: 'I will show that Smallest a thing or two when he comes up. He is keen-stuff.'

Time whiles after that, Shiny Plate got up strong, and made-sing. Adar looked out from high up, and said: 'Quiet!' We played Rattle-chain round our kennels. Adar said: 'Drat!' She came and unloosed, like she always does when we do enough. We went for walkabouts in Gardens and Orchard like we always do when she does. It were fun. Then we heard 'Lost Hound' like long ways off, but not proper singing. We said: 'Who is? Come here.' It said: 'I do not know where "here" is. I do not see.' I said: 'That is Ravager. Rabbit it!' We rabbited through Orchard. There was Ravager. *But* he walked side-ways, head-twisty – very dretful. I said loud. He did not know. He said: 'I will go quick to Kennels.' But he went round and round. He said: ''Ware Kennel-that-Moves!' Slippers said: 'It is strange new 'stemper-dog inside Ravager. 'Same what Cookey gave me egg-an'-brandy-for.' Ravager said: 'Where is my own place on the Bench?' But he bumped trees and twisted. We were afraid. We came each one side him. We came to own kennels… He fell down between. We licked his head because it were bleedy. After long whiles he said: 'Where is this?' We said: 'This is Boots and Slippers.' He tried to go away to Kennels. He could not lift. We lay close and licked and licked till Adar pulled back kitchen curtains for brekker. We said. She came quick. (Cookey too.)

There was egg-an'-brandy, as-fast-as-you-can. Master-Missus and Smallest came quick after. James went in Kennel-that-Moves to get Vet-Peoples out-of-bed-by-his-hair. Moore and Magistrate came quick too, because Ravager had not cast up at Kennels last night, and Upstart had fought Egoist for Ravager's place on sleepy-bench, and Kennels was all-of-a-nuproar. Moore said small to Ravager, but Ravager did not say back. Moore and Master put him on potting-bench in shed after Harry-with-Spade had broomed out and got small stove lighted. Smallest was took away to brekker, saying loud. Vet-Peoples did dretful things to Ravager's head. There was put-him-to-bed after. Moore set away straw same as at Kennels. Ravager tail-thumped two small times. We was let lie. We licked and we licked his head. Vet said he had lost one eye for always and not-much-chance for other. He said it were some-dash-motor. *And* Ravager were sick dog!

All those whiles, Smallest came to sit with, 'cept only when Guvvy took away or it was rides in Park. Me too, except if Master wanted me help him walkabout farms. One time I saw Tags in Wood Edge. I told about Ravager. He said: 'I knew it the same night. It were that kennel-that-moves of the nice-kind-ladies in the Cotswold country, which takes hens to be killed. Tell Ravager I am dash-sorry; because eyes are worse than legs. Tell him to come over some day when it is leaves-on, and we will talk old runs. We are both finished now; and no-bad-feelings.' And he said: 'Licking is best for cuts. Look at my toes!' And he said he was killing again off nice-kind-hen-killer-ladies, which was sending bill to the Cotswold *and* Heythrop. He said they was Prize Cockerels, but it were dash-difficult to get bellyful these hard late frosts. I said: 'There is fine dustbin at our place. I can lift lid with nose. We will not tell.' Tags said me: 'If your legs was good as your heart, I could not live for three fields in front of you. I am ashamed – 'my-time-of-life' – to go dust-binning. But I will come. Tell Ravager not to make a song about it, if he winds me.' So he came to our dustbin all quiet.

Whiles after that, Ravager was unsick Hound again. He said he had had thorn in foot at end of that run. He turned out on grass to bite it out, by gate of nice-kind-ladies where Tags killed chickens. Ladies was taking hens to be killed, lots-and-plenty, in kennel-that-moves. They skidded kennel on grass because they talked. They hit him into ditch, and he was made into strange blind dog. I told him about Tags and dustbin. He said: 'That is all proper. Tell him to come and talk me old runs together, because we are both out-of-it now.'

Time whiles after that, Ravager got down off bench and ate grass. He said me: 'I will go to my Kennels and speak them all there. Come with, because I do not see except my near side, and dash-little there.' Slippers said: 'It is riding-times for my Smallest. I will wait.' So I wented with Ravager. I put me his offside in case if he bumped. We wented slow up middle of Park, which he knew by nose. Kennels was shut. Moore and Magistrate was coming to take Smallest for ride. Proper Man were there too, with new-four-year-old. I sat down outside, because I do not like those dash new Hunt Terriers. Ravager put up nose and said very long at Kennel Gates. There was dretful noise inside Kennels, all together, one time, and stop. Proper Man said Moore: 'I did not think this would have to happen.' Moore said: 'I saw it once when I was stable boy to the Marquis, me Lord.' Proper Man said: 'Let him in and get it over, 'Pity's sake!' Ravager was let go in. He went to window looking into Hounds' sleepy-bench. He lifted himself up slow on sill, and looked them with his near eye. He did not say. There was one time more dretful noise inside, together, and stop. Then he *did* say very long, same as Lost Hound. Then he looked in, and 'was one more dretful cry inside. He dropped down. He came out. I said: 'What is?' He said: 'Upstart has my place on bench. I will go riding with Smallest.' Proper Man said Moore: 'Come *on!*' But Magistrate's girths was slack. Moore tighted up very careful. Proper Man blew his nose angry and said: 'You are as big dash-fool as your Master.' We

126

wented back to Smallest. Proper Man told Smallest Ravager would not ever come to Kennels any more, and gave him for very own to keep always. Master-Missus put in old Labrador Kennels by vegetable gardens, with day-and-night-bench, but never locked, so he could come and go like-he-felt. (I can open that with my nose too.)

After that, 'was plenty ridings in Park, because Magistrate had thick-leg and wanted gentle-summer-exercise. Those times, Smallest said all about real hunting, same as always. Moore said, if Ravager could speak, he could show Smallest more than Master-or-Me. He said all about real-hunts and Ravager, and Romeo and Regan, and Royal and Rachel, and Rupert and Ristori, which was all Ravager's fathers and mothers; and Foxes and Scents and casting hounds, and those fine things. Smallest found small red rumpet in Old Nursery, and played it were Horn-on-a-fine-hunting-morn. Moore showed how to squeak with. Ravager showed Slippers and me how to answer to Horn same as Sporting Pack. It were fun.

'Was one time when leaves-was-all-on, Shiny Plate came up strong and made-sing. We played Rattle-chain till Adar loosed, like she always does. We went to see Ravager, like we always do then. 'Was Tags outside old Labrador Kennels downwind under gooseberries, like he does when he comes for talk. There was big say-and-say about old runs with Ravager and Tags. They did not say same about things. Slippers said: 'No use worrying dead rats.' Ravager said: 'Better worrying dead rats than no rats ever.' Slippers said: 'I know a good rat. Make a new run by your two selves. Make a run for my Smallest.' Ravager said: 'He will come up with the young entry for cubbing in September. He will learn soon enough then.' Slippers said: *But* show him a run now by yourselves; because you and Tags are dash-cunning at both ends of the game.' Tags said: 'That looks like sound Rabbit. Bolt him.' Slippers said: 'Make my Smallest a play-hunt up and down Wood Edge

Rides. That Taffy is all grass-belly. He cannot jump, but he can wiggle through anywhere. Make a play-hunt up and down all Wood Rides.' I said: '*And* across Park, and plenty checks for me to keep with Ravager in case if he bumps.' Ravager said: 'I will not bump. I know every inch of the Park by nose. I will not bump.' Tags said: 'I am lame. I am fat. I am soon going to Brecknock.' Ravager said: 'You are too much dustbin. 'Do you good to have a spin in the open before you leave. 'Do us both good.' Tags said. 'That is Shiny-Plate-talk.' *But* he waggled his brush. Ravager said: 'What about scent this time-of-year?' Slippers said: 'Make it point-to-point, same as Hunt Races, and dash-all-scents.' Ravager said: 'But I must show our Smallest how proper hounds work. He must see a-little-bit-of-all-sorts.' Tags said: 'My toes tell me that when Shiny Plate sits down this morning, rain will come, and scent will lie.' Ravager said: 'You ought to know. Now, worry out run for Smallest.' So there were proper worry – like all shaking same rat – about line-of-country for Smallest's play-hunt. It were across Park from Wood's Edge Rides by Cattle Lodge and Little Water to Starling Wood, and saying goodbye to all kind friends at The Kennels, and finish at Made Earth's by Stone Wall on County road, because, Tags said, that were his back door to the Berkeley Country for Wales. Slippers and me helped lots. Then rain came, like Tags' toes said.

Morning-time 'was finished raining. Moore came with Magistrate – which had thick-leg and smelly bandage – only-for-gentle-work. Smallest took rumpet with, and own cracky whip, same as always. Ravager ran nearside Taffy. Me too. We wented up by Micefields to Middle Ride because of soft going, Moore said. In Middle Ride 'was Tags waiting like he said he would. Moore said: 'Dash his impertininces! Look at him!' Ravager gave tongue and wented up Ride. Me too. Smallest sticked hand behind ear and squealed proper. Tags scuttled limpity, but dash-quick. Magistrate see-sawed like that thing in Old Nursery. Moore said: ''Old 'ard you silly summer fool, you! Come back, Master Digby!' Smallest said: 'Hike to Ravager! Forrard on!' We rabbited down Middle Ride – 'normous long way. Tags turned right-handed into cover at Keeper's Oak, so he could slip into Park by Beech Hedge Gaps and Three Oaks, like he said he would. It were thick cover. We took it easy because it were hot. I keeped beside Ravager because he did not see. Tags said him in cover: 'There is nothing wrong with your legs.' Ravager said: ''Sorry if I pressed! I know Middle Ride by nose. That were not bad beginning.' Moore said loud: 'Come away, Master Digby. You won't see any more of him. He'll be through all manner of counties by now.' Smallest said: 'Don't you hunt my hounds!' Taffy pecked on anthill in fern. Smallest pitched forward and hit face on Taffy's head. His nose bleeded plenty. He wiped with hand across. Moore said: 'What *will* I say to your Ma?' Slippers said: 'Ravager, draw down West Ride, where that Taffy can see his stoopid feet!' Ravager spoke, and drew down West Ride over turf all proper, to Beech Hedge Gaps into Park by Three Oaks. Taffy wiggled through. Magistrate after. *He* were like bullocks. Moore was all leafy. He bad-worded Magistrate. Tags came out from behind Three Oaks like he said he would, and wented down Little Water. Smallest rumpeted. Moore said: 'He ain't ever going to cross the Park? Or *is* he? Dash if I make-it-out-at-all!' Tags went by Little Water to Park Dingle. He crossed Water two times, like he said he would, and went along from Park Dingle to Larch Copse.

Ravager took up scent and worked along Little Water quite slow, to show Smallest proper-good-work. Moore said: 'Watch, Master Digby! You'll never see anything prettier in your life – young as you are!' It were dretful strong scent. Slippers and me spoke to it loud. Ravager too. When we came to Larch Copse, where Tags had doubled, like he said he would, Ravager said: 'Stop it, stoopids! We lose the Scent here.' He threw up head, and went back to Taffy and Smallest, and sat down and scratched ear. (Slippers and me too.) Smallest said: 'Shall I cast them?' Moore said: ' 'Can't have it both ways, Master Digby. They're your 'ounds, not mine.' Smallest put finger in mouth and bited, like he does when he does not know. Moore did not say. We did not say. After whiles (we did not say) Smallest rumpeted, and cast back other side Little Water to Park Dingle. Ravager said: 'Our Smallest is no fool!' We all worked hard on back-cast. Slippers said: 'May I give tongue now for my Smallest? Scent is strong enough to kill pigs.' So he were let give tongue. (Me too.) Ravager confirmed. Tags got out of Park Dingle like he said he would. We all rabbited for Cattle Lodge in Park, where once fat Bull was which we hunted. It were sound turf which Ravager knew by nose. That were f'rocious Burst. I led Slippers to Lodge. Tags got under yard gate. Ravager said me: 'May I fly cattle-bars? I think the top one is down.' I said: 'It is up. Go under!' He were dretful ashamed, but he did go under. We all sat in calf shed, where water trough is, and drinked. We were thirsty. After whiles, Moore said to Smallest outside: 'What made you cast back at Larch Copse, sir?' Smallest said: 'If I were lame Fox pushed out of my Woods, I would try to get back.' Moore said: ' 'Eaven be praised! You have it in you! I 'ave only 'elped fetch it out!' Tags said Ravager: 'It is time I left the country. Was anything wrong with my double? Did either you little 'uns give that cub of yours a lead about it?' Slippers said: 'I *did* try to help my Smallest by edging off. But he was angry, and told me off proper. That back-cast were all his own rat.' Then Tags said Ravager: 'Why did you run so mute down Little Water? Young 'uns are always keen on music, you know.' Ravager said: 'Sorry! That was my Mother's fault, too, on a scent. She always preferred her work to her company. Same as me.' Tags said: 'Come on, then. Next point is Starling Wood. I shall work down old Drainage Ditch, taking it easy, and slip in by Duck's Hollow. It will be more little-bit-of-all-sorts for your Smallest.'

Tags broke to view behind Cattle Lodge, like he said he would. There were scurry over turf to Old Ditch. He dropped in. It were deep – with brambles. We took it easy. Smallest said loud, because he could not see. Moore said: 'They are working their hearts out for you in there, Master Digby. Don't press 'em. Don't press!' Ravager said Tags: 'Show a bit, now and then. The Young Entry are all for blood, you know.' So Tags showed up two-three-times edge of ditch. *And* Smallest squealed and was happy-pup. At Ditch-end Tags said: 'Come through Duck's Hollow quiet, and 'ware new hurdles.' So we did. Starling Wood was hurdled tight. Ravager took hurdles flying skew-ways, because he saw them a little. I were uncomfy of my friend Ravager. I did not know what he would fall on – same as me with lawnmower and the pheasant bird. But it were only thistles. He said: 'Sorry! I forgot I were blind dog.'

We all sat. It were stinky, eggy, feathery birdy place – all sticks. Ravager said Tags: 'Moore never puts hounds in here. We do not like it, and Scent don't lie.' Tags said: 'But Moore does, and Foxes cannot be dash-particular.' Moore and Smallest came riding outside. We sat still. Moore said: 'He *can't* be there, Master Digby! No fox uses where starlings use. The Hounds won't look at Starling Wood.' Smallest said: 'You said hunting is what-can't-happen happenin' dash-always.' Moore said: 'Yes, but he's gone on to make his point across the Park. Come 'ome and wash your face 'fore any one sees.' Smallest said: 'And lose my Fox?' Moore said: 'Then get 'old of 'em and cast forward.' Smallest did not say. He took rumpet off his saddle and held out to Moore. Moore would not take. He wented over all red in his face. He said: 'I most 'umbly apologise, Master Digby. I do indeed.' Slippers said: 'I do not know this rat.' Ravager said: 'He is giving his horn to Moore, because Moore knows so dash-well how to find his fox.' Tags said Ravager: ''Better speak a little, or Moore will lose me – same as last season.' Ravager speaked. Smallest said: 'He *is* there! Ravager can't lie. You said so yourself. Get downwind quick!' Moore wented. He hit Magistrate proper. Slippers said: 'Why did Moore not take my Smallest's rumpet?' Ravager said:

'Moore is too dash-ashamed of himself for trying to hunt another man's hounds – same as that snipey-nose-man which The Master gave his horn to, because he said he was whip to the Bathsheba Lady-Pack.' Tags said Slippers: 'Come with! Here is another bit-of-all-sorts for your Smallest.' They wented where wood was stinkiest. Big cub ran out under hurdles at Smallest. Slippers after. Smallest did not like. He said: 'Fresh fox! 'Ware cub! Hike back to Ravager, you dash-lapdog!' And cut at Slippers with cracky-whip. *And* hit. Slippers came back quick. He said Tags had said him to-push-out-that-youngster-and-see-how-Smallest-took-it. Moore came round cover. Smallest said: 'I have bad-worded Slippers. I have cut at my own Slippers!' Moore said: 'Don't take that to heart! You can bad-word everyone at cover-side 'cept your own Pa-an-Ma and The-Master-an'-Me.' Tags said: 'I think I will start for Fan Dringarth tonight. This is going to be dash-poor country for cripples next season.' Ravager said: 'Have a heart! Stay and keep me company.' Tags said: 'I would, but I have only one brush. Now, next point is Made Earths at Stone Wall on County road, where I go under for Dean Forest. Ravager said: 'Made Earths is tight as drainpipes. You cannot get-away-out-of till dark.' Tags said: 'Drainpipes heave in frost. Then Badgers work 'em. But first we say farewell to all kind friends at The Kennels. There will be check at New Firs. You little 'uns drop out there, and take it easy up to Fir Knoll, till we come back from Long Dip. Then join in for rattling finish.'

Slippers said: 'That Taffy cannot gallop to keep himself warm.' Ravager said: '*But* Magistrate wants three-new-legs. We will take care of them. Now play proper Pack. Get away together!'

Tags broke under Taffy's nose. 'Was most beautiful cry, and Adar could have covered with sheets. After that I were not so quick as Ravager. It were falling ground and sound turf, which Ravager knew by nose. 'Was nice check at New Firs, like Tags said. Slippers and me dropped out. Presently whiles, Tags broke to view down Long Dip. Ravager on his brush. It were real business. Slippers and me wented to Fir Knoll and watched. Taffy and Smallest was littler and littler in Long Dip. Moore and Magistrate too. Tags and Ravager was littlest, farest ways off, by Summer Kennels Yard. We heard Ravager speak most beautiful outside there. 'Was dretful common noises in Summer Kennels – like common dogs which cannot hunt when they want. I were happy-dog, because I do not like Upstart and Egoist. Nor new Hunt Terriers. (Slippers too.) We danced and singed.

Presently after whiles, Tags came up from Long Dip to Fir Knoll, dragging brush very limpity. He said: 'I am Sinking Fox! Ravager is Lost Hound! Taffy is cooked! Magistrate is fit-to-boil! Come along, little 'uns, and Devil-take-short-legs!' We rabbited. That were t'rific Burst. I headed Ravager for little whiles. We came to Made Earths screaming for blood. Tags got to ground in front of Ravager's front teeth, which was like rat traps. We all wented singing down into the dark. We sat, tongues-out. Ravager said: 'Top-hole finish!' Tags said: 'Not bad, our-time-of-life. That last point was quite a mile.' Ravager said: 'I make the run four mile from start to finish. You are too good for those Welshmen. Keep with us.' Tags said: 'Not with that youngster coming on. *But* he is Sportsman. Hark to him!' 'Was Smallest outside and Taffy blowing. Smallest said loud: 'He were lame! Don't let them get him! He are lame! Call 'em off, Moore, an' we'll look for that dash-cub.' And he rumpeted plenty. Moore said: 'We 'ave done enough for one July day, Master Digby. 'Ere's 'is Lordship coming, and I'll never 'ear the last of it.' Tags said Ravager: 'I think you will be wanted for hunting out of season. I am going to Wales. You are true Sporting Lot.' And Tags backed into Made Earths, which are his road to his home-among-the-rocks, where drain tiles was heaved up and Badgers helped, like he said he would, till we could not see his eye-shine any more. Ravager called after: 'You are best of them all, Tags!' But Tags did not say back.

We wented outside. There was Proper Man on Tall Horse coming slow from Kennels. Ravager said: 'He is not our Master now. Play proper Pack.' We lay down round Taffy, which was shaking tail, and girths-loosed, and Smallest making-much-of. Ravager did head-on-paws, and looked Smallest. I did thorn-in-foot. Slippers did burrs-in-tail. Moore did feeling Magistrate's thick-leg, and brushing leaves out of his front. Proper Man came up slow. He took off cap to Smallest. He said: 'Bowfront Hunt, I presume. 'Trust your Grace is satisfied with am-nities of my country.' Smallest said: ''Gone to ground. But it were spiffing run. I hunted own hounds. Listen, Uncle!' And he said and he said, like he can, about things, from find-to-finish. Proper Man said Moore: 'When you have quite done bot'nizing all over your belly, p'raps you will let me know.' Moore said: 'My fault, me Lord. All my fault. I 'aven't a shadow of an excuse. I was whip to one lame fox, one blind 'ound, two lapdogs, and a baby! And it was the run of me life. A bit-of-all-sorts, as you might say, me Lord, laid out as if it was meant to show Master Digby *multum-in-parvo,* so to speak. And may I never 'unt again, me Lord, if it 'asn't made 'im!' Proper Man said: 'Let's have every last yard of it.' Moore said and said: Smallest said and said, all one piece mixed. Proper Man asked about Tags' double, and Smallest's back-cast, and Scent and Starling Wood, and all those things, lots-and-plenty. He said it were babes-and-sucklings. We did not say. We tail-thumped when names was said, but no dash-parlour-tricks. We was proper Pack.

'Middle of say-so, Kennel-that-Moves came down County road with Missus, which had been shoppings. She stopped and overed wall in one. She came quick. She said: 'Digby! *Look* at your face!' Smallest said: 'Oh, I forgot, Taffy pecked and pitched me forward.' She said: 'In you get with me, and have it washed off.' Smallest said: 'Oh, Uncle!' Proper Man said: 'Let him take his hounds home, Polly. He has earned it.' Missus said: 'Then I will take Boots and Slippers. *They* don't hunt.'

But we would not. She said James said. Smallest did not say. *So* we would not go in Kennel-that-Moves. We wented all across Park with Ravager and Smallest and Taffy and Moore and Magistrate and Proper Man to Own Kennels – like proper Pack.

TOBY DOG

Please, this is only me-by-selfs. This is Boots which were friend of Ravager. I make Beseech… I tell. But I do not understand.

'Was time when Smallest went to Flat-in-Town for things-in-throat, which Vet-People cut out so he could sleep shut-mouth, and not ever catch cold. He said he would be dretful-good if we came after. So we wented with our Adar in dog-box-in-train. Guard People said we was Perfect Gentlemen.

Flat-in-Town were stinky. Smallest were sick-abed. Times after, he lay on couch-by-window-at-back which looks into garage-place. We sat in window because of cats.

One time 'was whistle-squeaky noises, and Frill Box, with legs under, came into garage-place. 'Was dog, like me and Slippers, with frilly collar. Plenty Smalls followed-tail. We told Smallest. He came to window in one. He said: 'Hooray! Punch-and-Judy!' Dirty Man, which was legs, came out from under Frill Box, and whistle-squeaked with things in front of teeth. Frill Dog walked with behind-legs and shaked hands with Smalls like Dirty Man told. Dirty Man went into Frill Box. Dollies came up on little sleepy-bench in front. One were all nose and bendy-back like which Smallest took off a Shiny-tree when he were pup. That Frill Dog came up on bench and bit Nose-Doll on nose. 'Was Scrap! Blue Dollie came. 'Was plenty Scraps! Nose-Doll put string round Blue Dollie and threw out over sleepy-bench and singed loud. 'Was finish. Dirty Man came out from under box, and showed his inside-hat to Smalls. They wented all away. He said: 'Garn! You spend fortuns on the movies, you do, but when it comes-to-drammer, you run-like-ares.' He whistle-squeaked and picked up Box and wented.

Time whiles after that, he came again. Smallest said James, which was up-with-the-washing: 'Take them down to see near-to.' We wented on-lead, and sat in front row. Frill Dog, which was called Toby Dog, did all those dash-parlour-tricks for Smalls again. We was ashamed, because he were same-like-us. We said. Toby Dog said back: 'If I weren't on-me-job, I'd give you something to sing for.'... James took away quick. Toby Dog said: 'Night-night! Don't choke yourselves, lovies!'

Time whiles more, Dirty Man came again. Smallest could not go down because of throat. James went and talked him plenty. Man said it were high-class-show-for-crowned-edds, but he would wash-hisself-first. James told Missus. *So,* Dirty Man came up to Flat, and 'was high-class-show for Smallest and all-us and our Adar. But Toby Dog were slow and sorrow-ful. Dirty Man said Missus, it were like-master-like-man, be-cause Toby Dog wore-hisself-out-giving-too-much-for-money, and he wanted rest-and-good-kind-home. That whiles, Toby Dog lay on back and rolled eyes like sick pup. Adar said: 'If those three get together, they will fight till dawn-o'-day! Look at Slippers's face!' Missus said did-not-know-quite-what-Master-will-say. James said he could keep in garage at home, so he could-not-come-into-contracts with anyone. *So,* 'was done, and Toby Dog was took down with James to be made well dog. Three-four daytimes after, we wented down in dog-box-train. Nice Guard-People said Adar we was fit-for-show-as-we-stood.

When we was home, we rabbited round borders for bones, which we had hid – in case of hungries. They was took – all! Slippers said 'It are that dash-Toby-Dog! C'm with, and house-train him!' We winded him in Wall Garden. We said loud. He did not say. He made his eyes ringy-white round edges. He putted his head under his front. He lifted up behind. He rolled behind-ends-over-heads. He rolled at us! First 'was whitey-eyes: then back-ends rolling at! We had never seen like *that*. It were vile undogful! But we did not run. When he rolled quite close, we went back. When he made singings like sick dog, we went back more quick to Own Gods on lawn. Master said me: 'Hullo, Boots! You look as if something had ruffled your self-esteem. What's the fuss?' I did not say. I helped him smoke-pipe like I always do. Harry-with-Spade came and said was rabbit in vegetable gardens. Master got two-bang-gun and went. We heeled quick. Toby Dog came out of garage, full-of-his-dash-self. He said: 'What is?' Slippers said: 'Come and see.' Slippers went into cabbages, and bolted rabbit, which are his 'complishment. Master fired over me and killed. Toby Dog went away like smoke. Master sent me to back door with rabbit to give our Adar, which are one of my 'complishments. We went-find Toby Dog. He were on tum in boot-box where James keeps shiny-feet-things. He said: 'What was? What was?' We said: 'Two-bang business.' He said: 'I cannot do! I am afraid! I can *not* do!' Slippers said: 'You are one dash-common-coward-thief-skug-dog! Where are bones?' Toby Dog told. We digged up and took which was left to old Labrador Kennel for safeness. We told Ravager. He were pleased of seeing us back. Toby Dog came round corner. He said: 'I may be skug-dog, but I am not fool. Let me in on your game, and I will let you in on mine.' Ravager said: 'What are your dirty game?' He said: 'Rats.' *And* he said he held rat-records at three pubz. We said: 'What are pubz?' He said: 'Lummy! You make me ache!' And he said pubz were where E went after 'is job. Slippers said: 'What are E?' Toby Dog said: 'Im-which-is-Own-God.' I said: 'What are job?' He said: 'What gets you your grub.' I said: 'That are our Adar when bell goes for Own Gods' Middle Eats; which are Lunch.' He said: 'You know fat lots, you do!' Ravager said: 'No scrappin'! Real-rat to Toby Dog. Job is same as business. After business is trough and sleepy-bench everywhere.' Slippers said: 'His business is dash-parlour-tricks.' And he said about Dirty Man and high-class-show. But he did not say about *that* in Wall Garden, which we had seen, because we was ashamed. Ravager said: 'Do parlour-tricks!' Toby Dog walked with behind-legs long whiles. He said there was not six-dogs-in-the-perfession like him. He said about rat-records which he held, which E, which were Own God, made betz on. And he said how James had taken him over to Walk when he came down, and Mister-Kent-Peoples brought plenty-rats to try-out. *And* he killed eight in half a minute on barn floor. He said James and Mister-Kent was dretful pleased, and was going-to-skin-the-village-alive as soon as odds-was-right. We did not understand.

Slippers said: 'If you are all this dash-fine-dog, why did Im push you off on James and Missus?' Toby Dog said: 'It is end of London season for Im. E don't need me awhile. So I play sick-dog and E sells me to nice-kind-people for good-'ome. Presently, E will come along and make whistle-squeak. I will hear and go back to me-job. P'raps it will be Frill Box and Dollies. P'raps it will be leading blind-man across Marble Arch.' Ravager said: 'Is E blind?' Toby Dog said: 'Blind-enough to get pennies-in-my-cup.' Ravager said: 'I am as near blind-as-makes-no-odds. I am sorry of E.' I told how Ravager had been blinded by nice-kind-hen-killer-ladies. Toby Dog said: 'If I had been along 'twould not have happened.' I were dretful angry. Ravager said: 'Drop it, Stoopid! Go and eat grass.'

So 'was walkabout in back gardens. Presently whiles, James brought cage of rats. And tipped out. I killed one. Slippers one. Toby Dog killed four which ran all different ways. James made-much-of, and said they would peel-the-breeches-off-the-village. Toby Dog were full-of-hisself. Slippers said: ''Ware two-bang-gun! Rabbit it, tripe-hound!' 'Was big say-and-say. Ravager came up from kennel. He said: 'What is silly-row *now?*' We told. Ravager sat and said: '*I* do not like two-bang-

139

guns, and my mother Regan did not. Toby Dog is *not* tripe-hound. He cannot help himself. It's same as you with swimming.' I said: 'We have long hairs and low-clearance, James says. Of course we do not like water.' Ravager said: ' 'Same with Toby Dog.' He told us off plenty for rudenesses, and went for sleep-in-fern near The Kennels in Park. Toby Dog said after: 'That is one proper-sort! That is real-true-dog-gent which I will not ever forget!'

'Was bell from house, which our Adar rings for us to help Smallest ride with Moore and Taffy. We rabbited. Toby Dog said: 'I come with.'

It were first ride after Flat-in-Town. 'Was bit-of-a-circus with Taffy because, Moore said, that bone-idle-stableboy had not exercised enough. But Smallest's legs was grown, and Taffy got-no-change. Smallest were a bit full-of-hisself. Moore said back: 'Don't be too proud, Master Digby! Seats-and-hands is Heaven's gifts.' Smallest were dretful 'shamed, because he *is* Champion Reserve Smallest. Moore said: 'Not but what you've good-right-to.' Ravager picked all us up in fern near The Kennels. Moore said: 'Ravager has been ailing ever since that motor hit him. I don't like it.' Ravager whimpered-to-name. Smallest said: 'Hush! He knows.' Moore said: 'There's not much he don't know.' And he said Ravager had took to lying-out-in-the-fern after Smallest went to Flat, so he could hear Hounds sing on Benches at morning-times for old-sake's-sake. Smallest said: 'Has Uncle Billy found out yet about Upstart?' Moore said: 'I told you too-much-for-your-age after our Lame Fox run. I 'ope you don't carry tales betwixt me and 'is Lordship.' Smallest said: 'Catch *me!* But I cannot ever be proper Master Foxhounds 'less you tell me all what you know?' Moore redded over front-of-face. He said: 'Thank you, Master Digby. When your time comes you'll 'ave to deal with such as Upstart. He has the looks-of-a-Nangel and the guts-of-a-mongrel.' And Moore said Rosemary did Upstart's work for him, which was great-granddaughter of Regan, and ran near-as-mute-as-the-old-lady. And he had watched Upstart at fault time and again, and Rosemary whimpering-in-his-ear to tip-him-the-office, and he taking-all-the-credit. And if, for-any-reason, she was not out, his second-string was Loiterer, which was a soft tail-hound, *but* with wonderful-tender-nose. And he had watched Upstart at a check play thorn-in-foot till Loiterer came up and put-him-wise. But he said, 'is Lordship was set on Upstart going to Peterborough, which are where Hounds go for Champion Reserves, and the pity was his looks-and-manners-made-it-a-cert. He said Upstart was born imposter, same as Usurper his sire, which-should-never-'ave-been, but 'is Lordship was misled by his looks, and would *not*-listen-to-advice. And he said Umbrage-his-Ma were a real-narsty-one on her-side-of-things. He said plenty-more-lots which I forgot. After pull-up, he said: 'Now, Master Digby, you have known the Hounds since you fell into the meal-bin in your petticoats. What do *you* think?' Smallest said: 'I could hunt any country in all the world with you and three couple which I were let choose. *And,* if Ravager were well-dog, I would make Uncle Billy present of the odd-couple.' Moore redded all fresh over face. He said: 'Lord love you! I shall be pushing-up-the-daisies long before that! But you 'ave it in you. You 'ave all three in you – Hound, Fox, and Horse! But, to get those three couple four-days-a-week, we have to put up with trash-like-Upstart.'

After whiles, 'was gallop. Slippers and Ravager went with. Toby Dog said me, sitting: 'That were rummy rat that man showed about that dash-clever dog. Tell again.' So I told about Upstart which I do not like, and how he got Musketeer help him fight Egotist for Ravager's place on sleepy-bench that night which Ravager did not cast up. And choked Musketeer after. *And* were glutton at the break-up-and-eat, which are not proper-game for lead-hounds, Ravager says, and did never go-in-for. Toby Dog said: 'It is cruel-ard on perfessional dog to be knocked out of his job for no fault of hisn, like that real-old-dog-gent of yours.' I said: 'You are not half-bad-dog.' He said:

'I am perfessional. I do not tell all I can do, *but* I will put you up to proper rattings.' So we wented to Walk and ricked round ricks. He showed how to chop rats – one-chop-one-rat, and not ever to shake, because it loses-time-on-the-count, he said. He told about rat-match at pub-in-village, where he were backed against Fuss, Third Hunt Terrier, which he said were pretty lady-dog which he could give ten rats in the minute and scratch-hisself-at-same-time.

Then we wented back to Labrador Kennel. Ravager was home and told us off proper for shirking-gallop. Slippers came too, because Smallest were at lesson. He said me he were pleased of Toby Dog not keeping with Smallest, because he did not want Smallest to care for. I said: 'That Toby Dog does not want Smallest. He is dash-clever dog, which does not do more *ever* than kill his rat. Leave alone!'

So 'was done. Toby Dog keeped with James about rats 'cept when he went rides with Smallest and us. One time Moore made that bone-idle-stableboy lay drag to teach Taffy jumps and ditches for cubbing-times. It were dustbin-herring-tails which I knew. Ravager said drags was stinkpot-stuff and wented home. (Me with.) So Toby Dog led. Time after that time, Smallest took him on lawn and said: 'Do tricks!' Toby Dog sat and scratched ears. Smallest smacked head and said: 'You are impostor like Upstart!' Toby Dog said us after: 'Catch me working overtime for anyone 'cept Im and your real-true-dog-gent!' He speaked plenty to Ravager about hunting and hounds and all those things because he said he were perfessional and wanted to know about Ravager's perfession. Ravager liked, and told plenty back. And Toby Dog showed me real rattings and the watch-two-while-you-kill one game. I sat out in fern with Ravager, which were my true friend since we was almost pups. And Smallest made Taffy jump-like-fleas, Moore said. *So* we was all happy dogs, that times.

Then 'was rat-match in village. Toby Dog said it were a cert, but he would give Fuss a look-in for looks' sake. That were night before Bell-Day, and strong Shiny Plate. Slippers and me did walkabouts in gardens waiting-for-result. (We are not tied up ever now since that man came over garden wall to see about the broccoli and were nipped on behinds going-back-over.) Toby Dog came home after match, which he had winned by what-you-dash-like. He said he had winded Dirty Man outside Spotted-Hound-pub in village. We said: 'What rat do you run now?' He said: 'E will need all day to sleep-it-off. E will come tomorrow night. I am glad, because E is Own God. *But* I am sorry, because you two and your true-old-gent-dog have done me well, and I ad-oped to pay all 'fore I sloped. But E is Own God. When E comes, I go with.' We said: 'Sorry too.' We all went walkabouts ('was hedgehogs) and sat.

Next daytime was Bell-Day and no-silly-weekend-visitors, Smallest said. We wented all for Middle Eats to Big House, where Proper Man lives, which are called Uncle Billy. Only 'cepting Ravager, which lay out in fern by the Kennels like always. Toby Dog had went to help James collect-debts-out-of-that-dash-swindling-stableboy about rat-match. So we did not see.

At Middle Eats was Master-Missus and Smallest and Proper Man and Proper Missus and my friend Butler, which I like, and a new Peoples which was called Jem, which was Master of some Hounds from some-place-else. 'Was plenty Own Gods' say-and-say about hounds-and-feet and those things. Smallest did not say, like he does not ever about Hounds. ('Cept to Moore.)

After coffee-sugar, my friend Butler asked me into laundry yard to help about rat-in-ivy. I chopped. ('Was cheese.) Butler made carrot-basket for all-Peoples to give Tall Horses. *So,* 'was walk-to-Kennels, which is always Bell-Day-rat after Middle Eats. I picked up Ravager in fern. He said: 'Run along with. I never go. I am no Hound any more.' I wented into yard with all-Peoples.

'Was Moore which called out Hounds by ones to stand for biscuit. 'Was plenty more say-and-say about legs-and-feet.

Smallest did not say, but all hounds speaked him small and soft on flags. That Master Jem said: 'Why, Diggy-boy, they seem to know you as well as Moore!' Smallest said back: 'How vewy odd!' because he does not like old Nursey-Thick-names casting-up. (Same as me when my Adar says 'Bootles'.) Missus said small: 'Digby! Behave!' Moore called out Upstart quick, and so 'was loud say-and-say about looks and manners and Belvoir-tans. (*We* played fleas-on-tum.)

Then Proper Missus put hand-before-front-teeth. *So,* all-Peoples went to see Tall Horses, 'cept Smallest and Moore. Then Toby Dog came round corner from Tall Horse Kennels, all small and dusty-looking. He said us, out of side-mouth: 'Lummy, what a swine! If he don't scare, I'm a goner. Head my rat!' He made his eyes ringy-white all round, like in Wall Garden. He putted down his head under, and hunched up all his behinds, and rolled himself that undogful way which we had seen. *But* worse! It were horrabel! Upstart uphackled. But we headed Toby Dog's rat. We singed: 'What is? Oh, we are afraid!' Toby Dog made screamy-draggly noise like cat-pups. And rolled *at!* Upstart bolted out of yard same as pup-for-cutty-whip, and bolted into fern where Ravager were. We heard plenty yowl-and-kai-yai. Toby Dog untinged his eyes, and was little cheap skug-dog, which walked away. All-Peoples at Horse Kennels came back and said loud about what-on-earth-was-the-matter-of-Upstart. Moore said seemingly-he-had-took-offence-at-the-terrier's-doings, and went-off-like-fireworks. That Master Jem said it were dretful-catching-fits, which play-deuce-and-all-with-Packs. Proper Man were angry. Smallest said: 'Won't he be all right for Peterborough, Uncle Billy?' Proper Man said: 'Dash Peterborough! Dash jackal! Never trust Usurper-blood, Moore! I warned you at the time.' Soon whiles, Upstart came back singing snuff-and-butter, Moore said. Moore did not like, and turned him into Kennels which did not like, because he were beaten-hound and telling-it. 'Was big Bench-scrap! Moore went in and rated proper. Smallest looked through window, where Ravager had looked when he came blinded. He said: 'Hooray! Musketeer has took Upstart's place and Upstart has Loiterer's – *right* at edge by door!'

Soon whiles, all-Peoples went back to tea saying say-and-say about fits. Smallest walked behind with Slippers and me. Time whiles he danced. We helped. We picked up Ravager in fern. I said: 'We heard. Did you get?' Ravager said: 'I could not help. He fell over me like blind dog. I got him across the loins and wrenched him on his back. But he was in a hurry. What began it?' I told all what Toby Dog had done to Upstart. Ravager said: 'That is a dash-odd-little-dog, but I like him. He hunts with his head. What was the Bench-row about afterwards?' I told how Upstart had lost bench-place to Musketeer and had been gived Loiterer's. Ravager said 'Good rat to Toby Dog! That place was colder than Cotswold when I was a young 'un. Now I am happy!' We wented all in, and plenty things under tea table. Ravager did not take. He sat by Proper Man, head-on-knee. Proper Man said: 'What's brought you back to your old 'legiance, old fellow? You belong to Digby now.' Ravager said soft and kissed hand. Proper Man said: ''Queer as his Mother before him!' After lots more say-and-say we all wented home 'cross Park. Smallest danced and singed loud till kennel-up. We went upstairs to help, like always when Guvvy lets. Ravager came with. That dash-Guvvy said him. Rudenesses on the stairs. Adar said her: 'Beg pardon, Miss, but no one ever questions the old gentleman's comings-and-goings in *this* house.' Ravager tail-thumped and kissed Smallest's two hands at pyjarm-time. He went downstairs slow, because he never-comes-up-to-the-top-landing. He said me: 'Now I am all-round-happy-hound. Come see me later, Stoopid. I've something to tell you.' I helped Master-Missus spend-happy-evening, like I do, till Adar came to take out and give night-bones.

After, I went for walkabouts with Slippers, because Shiny Plate were shiny-strong. James came and called Toby Dog, which he could not find. *And* dashed and wented. Toby Dog came out behind rhubarb-pots. He asked about Upstart. We told. He were happy dog. He said he had near-given-Alsatians fits-that-way. He asked if old true-gent-dog Ravager were pleased of his doings. He said he could not go-see him, because he were on-dooty expecting Im which was Own God any minute now. *And* he said he were plenty skug-cur about that two-bang business which were not perfessional. We said he were wonderful brave dog about Upstart, which me and Slippers would not have taken on. He said: 'Fairy Ann! Fairy Ann!' *But* he were most-happy dog. Presently whiles 'was whistle-squeak down lane by Orchard. Toby Dog said: 'That's Im. S'long!' He wented all little through hedge. Dirty Man said outside: 'Oh! You've come, 'ave yer? Come orn!'

Please, that is finish all about Toby Dog, which Ravager liked. (Me too.)

Slippers went-to-bone. I wented Labrador Kennel to speak Ravager, and opied door with my nose like I can.

Ravager said: 'Who is?' I said: 'Boots.' He said 'I know that, but Who Else came in with?' I said: 'Only Boots.' He said: 'There *is* Someone-else-more! Look!' I said: 'Toby Dog has gone back to Im. Slippers has kennelled-up. It is only me-by-selfs. But I am looking.' 'Was only Ravager and me everywhere. Ravager said: 'Sorry! I am getting blinder every day. Come and sit close, Stoopid.' I jumped on sleepy-bench, like always, night-times. He said: 'Sit closer. I am cold. Curl in between paws, so I can lay head-on-back.' So 'was.

Presently whiles, he said: 'If this black frost hold, goodbye hunting.' I said: 'It is warm leaves-on night, with Shiny Plate and rabbits-in-grass.' He said: 'I'll take your word for it,' and put head on my back, long whiles all still. Then he said: 'I know now what it was I meant to tell you, Stoopid. Never wrench a hound as heavy as yourself at my time of life. It plays the dickens with your head and neck.' *And* he hickied. I said: 'Sick-up, and be comfy.' He said: 'It is not tum-hickey. It is in throat and neck. Lie a bit closer.' He dropped head and slept. Me too. Presently whiles, he said: 'Give me my place on the Bench or I'll have the throat out of you!' I said: 'Here is all own bench and all own place.' He said: 'Sorry! I were with the old lot.' Then he dropped head-on-me and sleep-hunted with hounds which he knew when he came up from Walk. I heard and I were afraid. I hunched-up-back to wake him. He said, all small, 'Don't go away! I am old blind hound! I am afraid! I am afraid of kennel-that-moves! I cannot see where here is!' I said: 'Here is Boots.' He said: 'Sorry! You are always true friend of Ravager. Keep close, in case if I bump.' He sleeped more, and Shiny Plate went on across over. Then he said: 'I can see! 'Member Bucket on my head? 'Member Cow-pups we was whacked for chasing-pounds-off? 'Member Bull-in-Park? I can see all those things, Stoopid. I *am* happy-hound! Sorry if I were a noosance!'

So he sleeped long whiles. Me too, next to chest between paws. When I unsleeped, Shiny Plate was going-to-ground, and hen-gents was saying at Walk, and fern-in-Park was all shiny. Ravager unsleeped slow. He yawned. He said, small: 'Here is one happy hound, with 'nother happy day ahead!' He shaked himself and sat up. He said loud: 'It is morning! Sing, all you Sons of Benches! Sing!' Then he fell down all-one-piece, and did not say. I lay still because I were afraid, because he did not say any more. Presently whiles, Slippers came quiet. He said: 'I have winded Something which makes me afraid. What is?' I said: 'It is Ravager which does not say any more. I am afraid, too.' He said: 'I are sorry, but Ravager is big strong dog. He will be all right soon.' He wented away and sat under Smallest's window, in case of Smallest singing-out at getting-up-time, like he always does. I waited till my Adar opened kitchen curtains for brekker. I called. She came quick. She said: 'Oh, my Bootles! Me poor little Bootles!' Ravager did not say her anything. She wented away to tell. I sat with, in case if he might unsleep. Soonwhiles, all-Peoples came – Smallest,

Master-Missus, and Harry-with-Spade. Slippers too, which stayed by his Smallest and kissed hands to make him happy-pup. They took up to Orchard. Harry digged and put under like bone. *But* it were my Ravager. Smallest said dretful loud, and they wented away – all – all – 'cept my Adar which sat on wheelbarrow and hickied. I tried to undig. She picked up, and carried to kitchen, and held me tight with apron over heads and hickied loud. They would not let me undig more. There was tie-up. After that whiles, I went for walkabouts, in case if p'raps I could find him. I wented to his lie-down in fern. I wented to Walk and Wood Ride and Micefield, and all those old places which was. He were not there. So I came back and waited in Orchard, where he cast up blinded that night, which were my true friend Ravager, which were always good to me since we was almost pups, and never minded of my short legs or because I were stoopid. *But* he did not come...

Please, this is finish for always about Ravager and me and all those times.

Please, I am very little small mis'able dog!... I do not understand!... I do not understand!

THE SUPPLICATION OF THE BLACK ABERDEEN

I pray! My little body and whole span
Of years is Thine, my Owner and my Man.
For Thou hast made me – unto Thee I owe
This dim, distressed half-soul that hurts me so,
Compact of every crime, but, none the less,
Broken by knowledge of its naughtiness.
Put me not from Thy Life – 'tis all I know.
If Thou forsake me, whither shall I go?

Thine is the Voice with which my Day begins:
Thy Foot my refuge, even in my sins.
Thine Honour hurls me forth to testify
Against the Unclean and Wicked passing by.
(But when Thou callest they are of Thy Friends,
Who readier than I to make amends?)
I was Thy Deputy with high and low –
If Thou dismiss me, whither shall I go?

I have been driven forth on gross offence
That took no reckoning of my penitence,
And, in my desolation – faithless me! –
Have crept for comfort to a woman's knee!
Now I return, self-drawn, to meet the just
Reward of Riot, Theft and Breach of Trust.
Put me not from Thy Life – though this is so.
If Thou forsake me, whither shall I go?

Into The Presence, flattening while I crawl –
From head to tail, I do confess it all.
Mine was the fault – deal me the stripes – but spare
The Pointed Finger which I cannot bear!
The Dreadful Tone in which my Name is named,
That sends me 'neath the sofa-frill ashamed!
(Yet, to be near Thee, I would face that woe.)
If Thou reject me, whither shall I go?

Can a gift turn Thee? I will bring mine all –
My Secret Bone, my Throwing-Stick, my Ball.
Or wouldst Thou sport? Then watch me hunt awhile,
Chasing, not after conies, but Thy Smile,
Content, as breathless on the turf I sit,
Thou shouldst deride my little legs and wit –
Ah! Keep me in Thy Life for a fool's show!
If Thou deny me, whither shall I go!...

Is the Dark gone? The Light of Eyes restored?
The Countenance turned meward, O my Lord?
The Paw accepted, and – for all to see –
The Abject Sinner throned upon the Knee?
The Ears bewrung, and Muzzle scratched because
He is forgiven, and All is as It was?
Now am I in Thy Life, and since 'tis so –
That Cat awaits the Judgement. May I go?

HIS APOLOGIES

Master, this is Thy Servant. He is rising eight weeks old.
He is mainly Head and Tummy. His legs are
uncontrolled.
But Thou hast forgiven his ugliness, and settled him on
Thy knee...
Art Thou content with Thy Servant? He is *very* comfy
with Thee.

Master, behold a Sinner? He hath done grievous wrong.
He hath defiled Thy Premises through being kept in too
long.
Wherefore his nose has been rubbed in the dirt, and his
self-respect has been bruiséd.
Master, pardon Thy Sinner, and see he is properly looséd.

Master – again Thy Sinner! This that was once Thy Shoe,
He hath found and taken and carried aside, as fitting
matter to chew.
Now there is neither blacking nor tongue, and the
Housemaid has us in tow.
Master, remember Thy Servant is young, and tell her to
let him go!

Master, extol Thy Servant! He hath met a most Worthy
Foe!

There has been fighting all over the Shop – and into the
   Shop also!
Till cruel umbrellas parted the strife (or I might have
   been choking him yet).
But Thy Servant has had the Time of his Life – and now
   shall we call on the vet?

Master, behold Thy Servant! Strange children came to
   play,
And because they fought to caress him, Thy Servant
   wentedst away.
But now that the Little Beasts have gone, he has returned
   to see
(Brushed – with his Sunday collar on –) what they left
   over from tea.

Master, pity Thy Servant! He is deaf and three parts
   blind,
He cannot catch Thy Commandments. He cannot read
   Thy Mind.
Oh, leave him not in his loneliness; nor make him that
   kitten's scorn.
He has had none other God than Thee since the year that
   he was born!

Lord, look down on Thy Servant! Bad things have come
   to pass,
There is no heat in the midday sun nor health in the
   wayside grass.
His bones are full of an old disease – his torments run and
   increase.
Lord, make haste with Thy Lightnings and grant him a
   quick release!

A SEA DOG[1]

When that sloop known to have been in the West Indies trade for a century had been repaired by Mr Randolph of Stephano's Island, there arose between him and her owner, Mr Gladstone Gallop, a deep-draught pilot, Admiral (retired) Lord Heatleigh, and Mr Winter Vergil, RN (also retired), the question how she would best sail. This could only be settled on trial trips of the above Committee, ably assisted by Lil, Mr Randolph's mongrel fox terrier, and, sometimes, the Commander of the HMS *Bulleana*, who was the Admiral's nephew.

Lil had been slid into a locker to keep dry till they reached easier water. The others lay aft watching the breadths of the all-coloured seas. Mr Gallop at the tiller, which had replaced the wheel, said as little as possible, but condescended, before that company, to make his boat show off among the reefs and passages of coral where his business and delight lay.

Mr Vergil, not for the first time, justified himself to the Commander for his handling of the great Parrot Problem, which has been told elsewhere. The Commander tactfully agreed with the main principle that – man, beast, *or* bird – discipline must be preserved in the Service; and that, so far, Mr Vergil had done right in disrating, by cutting off her tail feathers, Josephine, *alias* Jemmy Reader, the West African parrot...

[1]See *Limits and Renewals:* 'A Naval Mutiny.'

153

He himself had known a dog – his own dog, in fact – almost born, and altogether brought up, in a destroyer, who had not only been rated and disrated, but also re-rated and promoted, completely understanding the while what had happened, and why.

'Come out and listen,' said Mr Randolph, reaching into the locker. 'This'll do you good.' Lil came out, limp over his hand, and braced herself against the snap and jerk of a sudden rip which Mr Gallop was cutting across. He had stood in to show the Admiral Gallop's Island whose original grantees had freed their Carib slaves more than a hundred years ago. These had naturally taken their owners' family name; so that now there were many Gallops – gentle, straight-haired men of substance and ancestry, with manners to match, and instinct, beyond all knowledge, of their home waters – from Panama, that is, to Pernambuco.

The Commander told a tale of an ancient destroyer on the China station which, with three others of equal seniority, had been hurried over to the East Coast of England when the Navy called up her veterans for the War. How Malachi – Michael, Mike, or Mickey – throve aboard the old *Makee-do,* on whose books he was rated as 'Pup', and learned to climb oily steel ladders by hooking his forefeet over the rungs. How he was used as a tippet round his master's neck on the bridge of cold nights. How he had his own special area, on deck by the raft, sacred to his private concerns, and never did anything one hair's breadth outside it. How he possessed an officers' steward of the name of Furze, his devoted champion and trumpeter through the little flotilla which worked together on convoy and escort duties in the North Sea. Then the wastage of war began to tell and... The Commander turned to the Admiral.

'They dished me out a new Volunteer sub for First Lieutenant – a youngster of nineteen – with a hand on him like a ham and a voice like a pneumatic riveter, though he couldn't pronounce "r" to save himself. I found him sitting on the wardroom table with his cap on, scratching his leg. He said to me, "Well, old top, and what's the big idea for tomowwow's agony?" I told him – and a bit more. He wasn't upset. He was really grateful for a hint how things were run on "big ships" as he called 'em. (*Makee-do* was three hundred ton, I think.) He'd served in Coastal Motor Boats retrieving corpses off the Cornish coast. He told me his skipper was a vet who called the swells "fuwwows" and thought he ought to keep between 'em. His name was Eustace Cyril Chidden; and his papa was a sugar-refiner…'

Surprise was here expressed in various quarters; Mr Winter Vergil adding a few remarks on the decadence of the New Navy.

'No,' said the Commander. 'The "old top" business had nothing to do with it. He just didn't know – that was all. But Mike took to him at once.

'Well, we were booted out, one night later, on special duty. No marks or lights of course – raining, and confused seas. As soon as I'd made an offing, I ordered him to take the bridge. Cyril trots up, his boots greased, the complete NO. Mike and I stood by in the chart room. Pretty soon, he told off old Shide, our Torpedo Coxswain, for being a quarter-point off his course. (He *was,* too; but he wasn't pleased.) A bit later, Cyril ships his steam-riveter voice and tells him he's all over the card, and if he does it again he'll be "welieved". It went on like this the whole trick; Michael and me waiting for Shide to mutiny. When Shide came off, I asked him what he thought we'd drawn. "Either a dud or a diamond," says Shide. "There's no middle way with that muster." That gave me the notion that Cyril might be worth kicking. So we all had a hack at him. He liked it. He did, indeed! He said it was so "intewesting" because *Makee-do* "steered like a witch", and no one ever dreamed of trying to steer CMBs. They must have been bloody pirates in that trade, too. He was used to knocking men about to make 'em attend. He threatened a stay-maker's apprentice (they were pushing all sorts of shore-muckings at us) for imitating his lisp. It was smoothed over, but the man made the most of it. He was a Bolshie before we knew what to call 'em. He kicked Michael once when he thought no one was looking, but Furze saw, and the blighter got his head cut on a hatch-coaming. *That* didn't make him any sweeter.'

A twenty thousand-ton liner, full of thirsty passengers, passed them on the horizon. Mr Gallop gave her name and that of the pilot in charge, with some scandal as to her weakness at certain speeds and turns.

'Not so good a sea-boat as *her!*' He pointed at a square-faced tug – or but little larger – punching dazzle-white wedges out of indigo-blue. The Admiral stood up and pronounced her a North Sea minesweeper. ''Was. 'Ferry-boat now,' said Mr Gallop. ''Never been stopped by weather since ten years.'

The Commander shuddered aloud, as the old thing shovelled her way along. 'But she sleeps dry,' he said. '*We* lived in a foot of water. Our decks leaked like anything. We had to shore our bulkheads with broomsticks practically every other trip. Most of our people weren't broke to the life, and it made 'em sticky. I had to tighten things up.'

The Admiral and Mr Vergil nodded.

'Then, one day, Chidden came to me and said there was some feeling on the lower deck because Mike was still rated as "Pup" after all his sea-time. He thought our people would like him being promoted to Dog. I asked who'd given 'em the notion. "Me," says Cyril. "I think it'll help delouse 'em mowally." Of course I instructed him to go to Hell and mind his own job. Then I notified that Mike was to be borne on the ship's books as Able Dog Malachi. I was on the bridge when the watches were told of it. They cheered. Fo'c'sle afloat; galley-fire missing as usual; *but* they cheered. That's the Lower Deck.'

Mr Vergil rubbed hands in assent.

'Did Mike know, Mr Randolph? He did. He used to sniff forrard to see what the men's dinners were going to be. If he approved, he went and patronised 'em. If he didn't, he came to the wardroom for sharks and Worcester sauce. He was a great free-fooder. But – the day he was promoted Dog – he trotted round all messes and threw his little weight about like an Admiral's inspection – Uncle. (He wasn't larger than Lil, there.) Next time we were in for boiler-clean, I got him a brass collar engraved with his name and rating. I swear it was the only bit of bright work in the North Sea all the War. They fought to polish it. Oh, Malachi was a great Able Dog, those days, but he never forgot his decencies...'

Mr Randolph here drew Lil's attention to this.

'Well, and then our Bolshie-bird oozed about saying that a ship where men were treated like dogs and *vice versa* was no catch. Quite true, if correct; but it spreads despondency and attracts the baser elements. You see?'

'Anything's an excuse when they are hanging in the wind,' said Mr Vergil. 'And what might you have had for the standing-part of your tackle?'

'*You* know as well as I do, Vergil. The old crowd – Gunner, Chief Engineer, Cook, Chief Stoker, and Torpedo Cox. But, no denyin', we *were* hellish uncomfy. Those old thirty-knotters had no bows or freeboard to speak of, and no officers' quarters. (Sleep with your Gunner's socks in your mouth, and so on.) You remember 'em, sir?' The Admiral did – when the century was young – and some pirate-hunting behind muddy islands. Mr Gallop drank it in. His war experiences had ranged no further than the Falklands, which he had visited as one of the prize crew of a German sailing ship picked up Patagonia-way and sent south under charge of a modern sub lieutenant who had not the haziest notion how to get the canvas off a barque in full career for vertical cliffs. He told the tale. Mr Randolph, who had heard it before, brought out a meal sent by Mrs Vergil. Mr Gallop laid the sloop on a slant where she could look after herself while they ate. Lil earned her share by showing off her few small tricks.

'Mongrels are always smartest,' said Mr Randolph half defiantly.

'Don't call 'em mongrels.' The Commander tweaked Lil's impudent little ear. 'Mike was a bit that way. Call 'em "mixed". There's a difference.'

The tiger-lily flush inherited from his ancestors on the main-land flared a little through the brown of Mr Gallop's cheek. 'Right,' said he. 'There's a heap differ 'twixt mongrel and mixed.'

And in due time, so far as Time was on those beryl floors, they came back to the Commander's tale.

It covered increasing discomforts and disgusts, varied by escapes frc.n being blown out of water by their own side in fog; affairs with submarines; arguments with pig-headed convoy captains, and endless toil to maintain *Makee-do* abreast of her work which the growing ignorance and lowering morale of the new drafts made harder.

'The only one of us who kept his tail up was Able Dog Malachi. He was an asset, let alone being my tippet on watch. I used to button his front and hind legs into my coat, with two turns of my comforter over all. Did he like it? He had to. It was his station in action. *But* he had his enemies. I've told you what a refined person he was. Well, one day, a buzz went round that he had defiled His Majesty's quarterdeck. Furze reported it to me, and, as he said, "Beggin' your pardon, it might as well have been any of *us,* sir, as him." I asked the little fellow what he had to say for himself; confronting him with the circumstantial evidence of course. He was *very* offended. I knew it by the way he stiffened next time I took him for tippet. Chidden was sure there had been some dirty work somewhere; but he thought a Court of Inquiry might do good and settle one or two other things that were loose in the ship. One party wanted Mike disrated on the evidence. They were the – '

'*I* know 'em,' sighed Mr Vergil; his eyes piercing the years behind him.

'The other lot wanted to find out the man who had tampered with the – the circumstantial evidence and pitch him into the ditch. At that particular time, we were escorting minesweepers – every one a bit jumpy. I saw what Chidden was driving at, but I wasn't sure our crowd here were mariners enough to take the inquiry seriously. Chidden swore they were. He'd been through the Crystal Palace training himself. Then I said, "Make it so. I waive my rights as the dog's owner. Discipline's discipline, tell 'em; and it may be a counter-irritant."

'The trouble was there had been a fog, on the morning of the crime, that you couldn't spit through; so no one had seen anything. Naturally, Mike sculled about as he pleased; but his regular routine – he slept with me and Chidden in the wardroom – was to take off from our stomachs about three bells in the morning watch (half past five) and trot up topside to attend to himself in his own place. *But* the evidence, you see, was found near the bandstand – the after six-pounder; and accused was incapable of testifying on his own behalf... Well, that Court of Inquiry had it up and down and thortships all the time we were covering the minesweepers. It was a foul area; rather too close to Fritz's coast. *We* only drew seven feet, so we were more or less safe. Our supporting cruisers lay on the edge of the area. Fritz had messed that up months before, and lots of his warts – mines – had broke loose and were bobbing about; and then our specialists had swept it, and laid down areas of their own, and so on. Any other time all hands would have been looking out for loose mines. (They have horns that nod at you in a sickly-friendly-frisky way when they roll.) But, while Mike's inquiry was on, all hands were too worked-up over it to spare an eye outboard.... Oh, Mike knew, Mr Randolph. Make no mistake. *He* knew he was in for trouble. The Prosecution were too crafty for him. They stuck to the evidence – the *locus in quo* and so on... Sentence? Disrating to Pup again, which

159

carried loss of badge-of-rank – his collar. Furze took it off, and Mickey licked his hand and Furze wept like Peter... Then Mickey hoicked himself up to the bridge to tell me about it, and I made much of him. He was a distressed little dog. You know how they snuffle and snuggle up when they feel hurt.'

Though the question was to Mr Randolph, all hands answered it.

'Then our people went to dinner with this crime on their consciences. Those who felt that way had got in on me through Michael.'

'Why did you make 'em the chance?' the Admiral demanded keenly.

'To divide the sheep from the goats, sir. It was time... Well, we were second in the line – *How-come* and *Fan-kwai* next astern and *Hop-hell,* our flagship, leading. Withers was our Senior Officer. We called him "Joss" because he was always so infernally lucky. It was flat calm with patches of fog, and our sweepers finished on time. While we were escorting 'em back to our cruisers, Joss picked up some wireless buzz about a submarine spotted from the air, surfacing over to the north-east – probably recharging. He detached *How-come* and *Fan-kwai* to go on with our sweepers, while him and me went look-see. We dodged in and out of fog-patches – two-mile visibility one minute and blind as a bandage the next – then a bit of zincy sun like a photograph – and so on. Well, breaking out of one of these patches we saw a submarine recharging – hatches open, and a man on deck – not a mile off our port quarter. We swung to ram and, as he came broadside on to us, I saw *Hop-hell* slip a mouldie – fire a torpedo -- at him, and my Gunner naturally followed suit. By the mercy o' God, they both streaked ahead and astern him, because the chap on deck began waving an open brolly at us like an old maid hailing a bus. That fetched us up sliding on our tails, as you might say. Then he said, "What do you silly bastards think you're doin'?" (He was Conolly, and some of his crowd had told us, ashore, that the brolly was his private code. That's why we didn't fire on sight, sir. – "Red" Conolly, not "Black".) He told us he'd gone pretty close inshore on spec the night before and had been hunted a bit and had to lie doggo, and he'd heard three or four big ships go over him. He told us where that was, and we stood by till he'd finished recharging and we gave him his position and he sculled off. He said it was hellish thick over towards the coast, but there seemed to be something doing there. So we proceeded, on the tip Conolly gave us... Oh, wait a minute! Joss' Gunner prided himself on carrying all the silhouettes of Fritz's navy in his fat head, and he had sworn that Conolly's craft was the duplicate of some dam' U-boat. Hence his shot. I believe Joss pretty well skinned him for it, but that didn't alter the fact we'd only one mouldie apiece left to carry on with...

'Presently Joss fetched a sharp sheer to port, and I saw his bow wave throw off something that looked like the horns of a mine; but they were only three or four hock bottles. *We* don't drink hock much at sea.'

Mr Randolph and Mr Gallop smiled. There are few liquors that the inhabitants of Stephano's Island do not know – bottled, barrelled, or quite loose.

The Commander continued.

'Then Joss told me to come alongside and hold his hand, because he felt nervous.'

The Commander here explained how, with a proper arrangement of fenders, a trusty Torpedo Cox at the wheel, and not too much roll on, destroyers of certain types can run side by side close enough for their captains to talk even confidentially to each other. He ended, 'We used to slam those old dowagers about like sampans.'

'You youngsters always think you discovered navigation,' said the Admiral. 'Where did you steal your fenders from?'

'That was Chidden's pigeon in port, sir. He was the biggest thief bar three in the Service. CMBs are a bad school... So, then, we proceeded – bridge to bridge – chinning all comfy. Joss said those hock bottles and the big ships walking over Conolly interested him strangely. It was shoaling and we more or less made out the set of the tide. We didn't chuck anything overboard, though; and just about sunset in a clear patch we passed another covey of hock bottles. Mike spotted them first. He used to poke his little nose up under my chin if he thought I was missing anything. Then it got blind thick, as Conolly said it would, and there was an ungodly amount of gibber on the wireless. Joss said it sounded like a Fritz tip-and-run raid somewhere and we might come in handy if the fog held. (You couldn't see the deck from the bridge.) He said I'd better hand him over my surviving mouldie because he was going to slip 'em himself henceforward, and back his own luck. My tubes were nothing to write home about, anyhow. So we passed the thing over, and proceeded. We cut down to bare steerage-way at last (you couldn't see your hand before your face by then) and we listened. You listen better in fog.'

'But it doesn't give you your bearings,' said Mr Gallop earnestly.

'True. Then you fancy you hear things – like we did. Then Mike began poking up under my chin again. *He* didn't imagine things. I passed the word to Joss, and a minute or two after, we heard voices – they sounded miles away. Joss said, "That's the hock-bottler. He's hunting his home channel. I hope he's too bothered to worry about us; but if this stuff lifts we'll wish we were Conolly." I buttoned Mike well in to me bosom and took an extra turn of my comforter round him, and those ghastly voices started again – up in the air this time, and all down my neck. Then something big went astern, both screws – then ahead dead slow – then shut off. Joss whispered, "He's atop of us!" I said, "Not yet. Mike's winding him to starboard!" The little chap had his head out of my comforter again, sniffin' and poking my chin... And then, by God! the blighter slid up behind us to starboard. We couldn't see him. We felt him take what wind there was, and we smelt him – hot and sour. He was

162

passing soundings to the bridge, by voice. I suppose he thought he was practically at home. Joss whispered, "Go ahead and cuddle him till you hear me yap. Then amuse him. I shall slip my second by the flare of his batteries while he's trying to strafe you." So he faded off to port and I went ahead slow – oh, perishing slow! Shide swore afterwards that he made out the loom of the brute's stern just in time to save his starboard propeller. That was when my heart stopped working. Then I heard my port fenders squeak like wet cork along his side, and there we were cuddling the hock-bottler! If you lie close enough to anything big he can't theoretically depress his guns enough to get you.'

Mr Gallop smiled again. He had known that game played in miniature by a motor launch off the Bahamas under the flaring bows of a foreign preventive boat.

'...'Funny to lie up against a big ship eavesdropping that way. We could hear her fans and engine-room bells going, and some poor devil with a deuce of a cough. I don't know how long it lasted, but, all that awful while, Fritz went on with his housekeeping overhead. I'd sent Shide aft to the relieving tackles – I had an idea the wheel might go – and put Chidden on the twelve-pounder on the bridge. My Gunner had the forward six-pounders, and I kept *Makee-do* cuddling our friend. Then I heard Joss yap once, and then the devil of a clang. He'd got his first shot home. We got in three rounds of the twelve, and the sixes cut into her naked skin at – oh, fifteen feet it must have been. Then we all dived aft. (My ewe-torpedo wouldn't have been any use anyhow. The head would have hit her side before the tail was out of the tube.) She woke up and blazed off all starboard batteries, but she couldn't depress to hit us. The blast of 'em was enough, though. It knocked us deaf and sick and silly. It pushed my bridge and the twelve-pounder over to starboard in a heap, like a set of fire-irons, and it opened up the top of the forward funnel and flared it out like a tulip. She put another salvo over us that winded us again. Mind you, we couldn't hear *that!* We felt it. Then we were jarred sideways – a sort of cow-kick, and I thought it was finish. Then there was a sort of ripping woolly *feel* – not a noise – in the air, and I saw the haze of a big gun's flash streaking up overhead at about thirty degrees. It occurred to me that she was rolling away from us and it was time to stand clear. So we went astern a bit. And that haze was the only sight I got of her from first to last!... After a while, we felt about to take stock of the trouble. Our bridge wreckage was listing us a good deal to starboard: the funnel spewed smoke all over the shop and some of the stays were cut; wireless smashed; compasses crazy of course; raft and all loose fittings lifted overboard; hatches and suchlike strained or jammed and the deck leaking a shade more than usual. *But* no casualties. A few ratings cut and bruised by being chucked against things, and, of course, general bleeding from the nose and ears. But – funny thing – we all shook like palsy. That lasted longest. We all went about shouting and shaking. Shock, I suppose.'

'And Mike?' Mr Randolph asked.

'Oh, *he* was all right. He had his teeth well into my comforter throughout. 'First thing after action, he hopped down to the wardroom and lapped up pints. Then he tried to dig the gas taste out of his mouth with his paws. Then he wanted to attend to himself, but he found all his private area gone west with the other unsecured gadgets. He was very indignant and told Furze about it. Furze bellows into my ear, "That's proof it couldn't have been him on the quarterdeck, sir, because, if ever anyone was justified in being promiscuous, *now* would be the time. But 'e's as dainty as a duchess."... Laugh away! – It wasn't any laughing matter for Don Miguel.'

' – I beg his pardon! How did you settle his daintiness?' said the Admiral.

'I gave him special leave to be promiscuous, and just because I laughed he growled like a young tiger... You mayn't believe what comes next, but it's fact. Five minutes later, the whole ship was going over Mike's court-martial once again. They were digging out like beavers to repair damage, and chinning at the top of their voices. And a year – no – six months before, half of 'em were Crystal Palace naval exhibits!'

'Same with shanghaied hands,' said Mr Gallop, putting her about with a nudge of his shoulder on the tiller and some almost imperceptible touch on a sheet. The wind was rising.

'...I ran out of that fog at last like running out of a tunnel. I worked my way offshore, more or less by soundings, till I picked up a star to go home by. Arguin' that Joss 'ud do about the same, I waited for him while we went on cutting away what was left of the bridge and restaying the funnel. It was flat calm still; the coast fog lying all along like cliffs as far as you could see. 'Dramatic, too, because, when the light came, Joss shot out of the fog three or four miles away and hared down to us clearing his hawsers for a tow. We *did* look rather a dung-barge. I signalled we were all right and good for thirteen knots, which was one dam' lie... Well... so then we proceeded, line-ahead, and Joss sat on his depth-charge-rack aft, semaphoring all about it to me on my fo'c'sle-head. He had landed the hock-bottler to port with his first shot. His second – it touched off her forward magazine – was my borrowed one; but he reported it as "a torpedo from the deck of my Second in Command!" She was showing a blaze through the fog then, so it was a sitting shot – at about a hundred yards, he thought. He never saw any more of her than I did, but he smelt a lot of burnt cork. She might have been some old craft packed with cork like a life-boat for a tip-and-run raid. *We* never knew.'

Even in that short time the wind and the purpose of the waves had strengthened.

'All right,' said Mr Gallop. 'Nothin' due 'fore tomorrow.' But Mr Randolph, under sailing orders from Mrs Vergil, had the oilskins out ere the sloop lay down to it in earnest. 'Then – after that?' said he.

'Well, then we proceeded; Joss flag-wagging me his news, and all hands busy on our funnel and minor running repairs, but all arguin' Mike's case hotter than ever. And all of us shaking.'

'Where was Mike?' Mr Randolph asked as a cut wave-top slashed across the deck.

'Doing tippet for me on the fo'c'sle, and telling me about his great deeds. He never barked, but he could chin like a Peke. Then Joss changed course. I thought it might be mines, but having no bridge I had no command of sight. Then we passed a torpedo-bearded man lolling in a lifebelt, with his head on his arms, squinting at us – like a drunk at a pub... Dead? Quite... You never can tell how the lower deck'll take anything. They stared at it and our Cook said it looked saucy. That was all. Then Furze screeched: "But for the grace o' God that might be bloody-all of us!" And he carried on with that bit of the Marriage Service – "I ree-quire an' charge you as ye shall answer at the Day of Judgement, which blinkin' hound of you tampered with the evidence *re* Malachi. Remember that beggar out in the wet is listenin'." 'Sounds silly, but it gave me the creeps at the time. I heard the Bolshie say that a joke was a joke if took in the right spirit. Then there was a bit of a mix-up round the funnel, but of course I was busy swapping yarns with Joss. When I went aft – I didn't hurry – our Chief Stoker was standing over Furze, while Chidden and Shide were fending off a small crowd who were lusting for the Bolshie's blood. (He had a punch, too, Cywil.) It looked to me – but I couldn't have sworn to it – that the Chief Stoker scraped up a knife with his foot and hoofed it overboard.'

'Knife!' the shocked Admiral interrupted.

'A wardroom knife, sir, with a ground edge on it. Furze had been a Leicester Square waiter or pimp or something, for ten years, and he'd contracted foreign habits. By the time I took care to reach the working party, they were carrying on like marionettes, because they hadn't got over their shakes, you see.... *I* didn't do anything. I didn't expect the two men Chidden had biffed 'ud complain of him as long as the Bolshie was alive; and our Chief Stoker had mopped up any awkward evidence against Furze. All things considered, I felt rather sorry for the Bolshie... Chidden came to me in the wardroom afterwards, and said the man had asked to be "segwegated" for his own safety. Oh yes ! – he'd owned up to tampering with the evidence. I said I couldn't well crime the swine for blackening a dog's character; but I'd reinstate and promote Michael, and the lower deck might draw their own conclusions. "Then they'll kill the Bolshie," says the young 'un. "No," I said, "CMBs don't know everything, Cywil. They'll put the fear of death on him, but they won't scupper him. What's he doing now?" "Weconstwucting Mike's pwivate awea, with Shide and Furze standing over him gwinding their teeth." "Then he's safe," I said. "I'll send Mike up to see if it suits him. But what about Dawkins and Pratt?" Those were the two men Cyril had laid out while the Chief Stoker was quenching the engine-room ratings. *They* didn't love the Bolshie either. "Full of beans and blackmail!" he says. "I told 'em I'd saved 'em fwom being hung, but they want a sardine supper for all hands when we get in." '

'But what's a Chief Stoker *doin'* on the upper deck?' said Mr Vergil peevishly, as he humped his back against a solid douche.

'Preserving discipline. Ours could mend anything from the wardroom clock to the stove, and he'd *make* a sailor of anything on legs – same as you used to, Mr Vergil.... Well, and so we proceeded, and when Chidden reported the "awea" fit for use I sent Mike up to test it.'

'Did Mike know?' said Mr Randolph.

'Don't ask me what he did or didn't, or you might call me a liar. The Bolshie apologised to Malachi publicly, after Chidden gave out that I'd promoted him to Warrant Dog "for conspicuous gallantwy in action and giving valuable information as to enemy's whaiwabouts in course of same". So

Furze put his collar on again, and gave the Bolshie *his* name and rating.'

The Commander quoted it – self-explanatory indeed, but not such as the meanest in His Majesty's Service would care to answer to even for one day.

'It went through the whole flotilla.' The Commander repeated it, while the others laughed those gross laughs women find so incomprehensible.

'Did he stay on?' said Mr Vergil. 'Because *I* knew a stoker in the old *Minotaur* who cut his throat for half as much as that. It takes 'em funny sometimes.'

'He stayed with us all right; but he experienced a change of heart, Mr Vergil.'

'I've seen such in my time,' said the Ancient.

The Admiral nodded to himself. Mr Gallop at the tiller half rose as he peered under the foresail, preparatory to taking a short cut where the coral gives no more second chance than a tiger's paw. In half an hour they were through that channel. In an hour, they had passed the huge liner tied up and discharging her thirsty passengers opposite the liquor shops that face the quay. Some, who could not suffer the four and a half minutes walk to the nearest hotel, had already run in and come out tearing the wrappings off the whisky bottles they had bought. Mr Gallop held on to the bottom of the harbour and fetched up with a sliding curtsey beneath the mangroves by the boat shed...

'I don't know whether I've given you quite the right idea about my people,' said the Commander at the end. '*I* used to tell 'em they were the foulest collection of sweeps ever forked up on the beach. In some ways they were. But I don't want *you* to make any mistake. When it came to a pinch they were the salt of the earth – the very salt of God's earth – blast 'em and bless 'em. Not that it matters much now. We've got no Navy.'

Rudyard Kipling

Captains Courageous

Harvey Cheyne is the spoilt, precocious son of an over-indulgent millionaire. On an ocean voyage off the Newfoundland coast, he falls overboard and is rescued by a Portuguese fisherman. Never in need of anything in his entire life, it comes as rather a shock to Harvey to be forced to join the crew of the fishing schooner and work there for an entire summer.

By being thrown into an entirely alien world, Harvey has echoes of Kipling's more famous Mowgli from *The Jungle Book*, and, like Mowgli, Harvey learns to adapt and make something of himself. *Captains Courageous* captures with brilliant detail all the colour of the fishing world and reveals it as a convincing model for society as a whole.

The Jungle Book

The Jungle Book is one of the best-loved stories of all time. In Mowgli, the boy who is raised by wolves in the jungle, we see an enduring creation that has gained near-mythical status. And with such unforgettable companions as Father and Mother Wolf, Shere Khan and Bagheera, Mowgli's life and adventures have come to be recognised as a complex fable of mankind. With a rich and vibrant imagination behind layer upon layer of meaning, Kipling has created a pure masterpiece to thrill and delight adult and child alike.

Rudyard Kipling

Many Inventions

Lo, this only have I found, that God hath made man upright; but they have sought out many inventions – Ecclesiastes vii v. 29

Here Kipling adds to the world's catalogue of inventions since the dawn of time with a few of his own notable examples. *Many Inventions* brings together a number of Kipling's short stories and includes such works as 'His Private Honour', 'Brugglesmith' and 'The Record Of Badalia Herodsfoot'. Embracing his eternal preoccupations of Anglo-Indian relations and human sufferings, this collection is a fine example of Kipling's entire work.

Plain Tales from the Hills

Plain Tales from the Hills is an outstanding collection of stories of colonial life capturing all the richness of India's sights, sounds and smells. The tales Kipling tells are ones of loss, suffering and broken faith, a far cry from the celebratory patriotism that surrounded the Empire at the time. He writes with haunting passion about the cultural, racial and sexual barriers of the day and the stories resound with a tender, yet tragic, poignancy.

RUDYARD KIPLING

REWARDS AND FAIRIES

Rewards and Fairies is a delightful selection of stories and poems from the creator of *The Jungle Book*. Tales of witches, looking-glasses and square toes come together with all the old favourites including 'The Way Through the Woods' to make a thoroughly enchanting book. And perhaps most famous of all, included in this collection is Kipling's well-loved poem, 'If' – words that have spoken to the hearts of many a generation.

UNDER THE DEODARS

Under the Deodars is a disturbing, uncomfortable and unsettling read – as Kipling himself said, 'it deals with things that are not pretty and ugliness can hurt'. For here, Kipling takes as his subject matter the life of Englishmen and women in the Indian Subcontinent, and explores the ugly truth of what went on beneath the appealing 'froth' of club life. Instantly rejected by many as being too harsh and too critical, *Under the Deodars* is in fact a brilliant portrait of Anglo-Indians, and their unforgiving impact upon the provincial society of Simla.

OTHER TITLES BY RUDYARD KIPLING AVAILABLE DIRECT
FROM HOUSE OF STRATUS

Quantity		£	$(US)	$(CAN)	€
	ANIMAL STORIES	6.99	11.50	15.99	11.50
	COLLECTED DOG STORIES	6.99	11.50	15.99	11.50
	THE DAY'S WORK	6.99	11.50	15.99	11.50
	DEBITS AND CREDITS	6.99	11.50	15.99	11.50
	THE JUNGLE BOOK	6.99	11.50	15.99	11.50
	JUST SO STORIES	6.99	11.50	15.99	11.50
	KIM	6.99	11.50	15.99	11.50
	LAND AND SEA TALES	6.99	11.50	15.99	11.50
	THE LIGHT THAT FAILED	6.99	11.50	15.99	11.50
	LIMITS AND RENEWALS	6.99	11.50	15.99	11.50
	MANY INVENTIONS	6.99	11.50	15.99	11.50
	THE NAULAHKA - A STORY OF EAST AND WEST	6.99	11.50	15.99	11.50
	THE PHANTOM RICKSHAW & OTHER EERIE TALES	6.99	11.50	15.99	11.50

ALL HOUSE OF STRATUS BOOKS ARE AVAILABLE FROM GOOD BOOKSHOPS
OR DIRECT FROM THE PUBLISHER:

Internet: www.houseofstratus.com including author interviews, reviews, features.

Email: sales@houseofstratus.com please quote author, title and credit card details.

OTHER TITLES BY RUDYARD KIPLING AVAILABLE DIRECT
FROM HOUSE OF STRATUS

Quantity	£	$(US)	$(CAN)	€
PLAIN TALES FROM THE HILLS	6.99	11.50	15.99	11.50
PUCK OF POOK'S HILL	6.99	11.50	15.99	11.50
REWARDS AND FAIRIES	6.99	11.50	15.99	11.50
THE SECOND JUNGLE BOOK	6.99	11.50	15.99	11.50
THE SEVEN SEAS	6.99	11.50	15.99	11.50
SOLDIERS THREE AND OTHER STORIES	6.99	11.50	15.99	11.50
STALKY & CO.	6.99	11.50	15.99	11.50
TRAFFICS AND DISCOVERIES	6.99	11.50	15.99	11.50
UNDER THE DEODARS	6.99	11.50	15.99	11.50
WEE WILLIE WINKIE AND OTHER STORIES	6.99	11.50	15.99	11.50

ALL HOUSE OF STRATUS BOOKS ARE AVAILABLE FROM GOOD BOOKSHOPS
OR DIRECT FROM THE PUBLISHER:

Hotline: UK ONLY: 0800 169 1780, please quote author, title and credit card details.
INTERNATIONAL: +44 (0) 20 7494 6400, please quote author, title and credit card details.

Send to: House of Stratus Sales Department
24c Old Burlington Street
London
W1X 1RL
UK

Please allow for postage costs charged per order plus an amount per book as set out in the tables below:

	£(Sterling)	$(US)	$(CAN)	€(Euros)
Cost per order				
UK	2.00	3.00	4.50	3.30
Europe	3.00	4.50	6.75	5.00
North America	3.00	4.50	6.75	5.00
Rest of World	3.00	4.50	6.75	5.00
Additional cost per book				
UK	0.50	0.75	1.15	0.85
Europe	1.00	1.50	2.30	1.70
North America	2.00	3.00	4.60	3.40
Rest of World	2.50	3.75	5.75	4.25

PLEASE SEND CHEQUE, POSTAL ORDER (STERLING ONLY), EUROCHEQUE, OR INTERNATIONAL MONEY ORDER (PLEASE CIRCLE METHOD OF PAYMENT YOU WISH TO USE)
MAKE PAYABLE TO: STRATUS HOLDINGS plc

Cost of book(s): ——————— Example: 3 x books at £6.99 each: £20.97

Cost of order: ——————— Example: £2.00 (Delivery to UK address)

Additional cost per book: ——— Example: 3 x £0.50: £1.50

Order total including postage: ——— Example: £24.47

Please tick currency you wish to use and add total amount of order:

☐ £ (Sterling) ☐ $ (US) ☐ $ (CAN) ☐ € (EUROS)

VISA, MASTERCARD, SWITCH, AMEX, SOLO, JCB:

☐☐☐☐☐☐☐☐☐☐☐☐☐☐☐☐☐☐☐☐

Issue number (Switch only):

☐☐☐

Start Date:

☐☐/☐☐

Expiry Date:

☐☐/☐☐

Signature:

NAME:

ADDRESS:

POSTCODE:

Please allow 28 days for delivery.

Prices subject to change without notice.
Please tick box if you do not wish to receive any additional information. ☐

House of Stratus publishes many other titles in this genre; please check our website (**www.houseofstratus.com**) for more details.